Order this book online at www.trafford.com/07-0613
or email orders@trafford.com

Most Trafford titles are also available at major online book retailers.

© Copyright 2008 Ashley Wincott.

All rights reserved. No part of this publication may be reproduced, stored in a retrieval system, or transmitted, in any form or by any means, electronic, mechanical, photocopying, recording, or otherwise, without the written prior permission of the author.

Note for Librarians: A cataloguing record for this book is available from Library and Archives Canada at www.collectionscanada.ca/amicus/index-e.html

Printed in Victoria, BC, Canada.

ISBN: 978-1-4251-2212-6

We at Trafford believe that it is the responsibility of us all, as both individuals and corporations, to make choices that are environmentally and socially sound. You, in turn, are supporting this responsible conduct each time you purchase a Trafford book, or make use of our publishing services. To find out how you are helping, please visit www.trafford.com/responsiblepublishing.html

Our mission is to efficiently provide the world's finest, most comprehensive book publishing service, enabling every author to experience success. To find out how to publish your book, your way, and have it available worldwide, visit us online at www.trafford.com/10510

www.trafford.com

North America & international
toll-free: 1 888 232 4444 (USA & Canada)
phone: 250 383 6864 ♦ fax: 250 383 6804
email: info@trafford.com

The United Kingdom & Europe
phone: +44 (0)1865 722 113 ♦ local rate: 0845 230 9601
facsimile: +44 (0)1865 722 868 ♦ email: info.uk@trafford.com

10 9 8 7 6 5 4 3 2

About the Author

Ashley Wincott is a life long cricket fan. Ashley's love of cricket dates back to his schooldays. He has played for Cropredy Cricket Club in Oxfordshire for over 35 years. He gained an ECB coaching qualification and helped set up a youth section at the club. This book is the culmination of an ambition to see his first book published.

Every effort has been made to ensure the accuracy of the facts and figures in this book.

There are so many friends and family I need to thank for their advice, support and encouragement in the writing of this book. You know who you are. My deepest thanks to you all.

My thanks to Patrick Eagar for his kind permission to reproduce the images on the front cover.

THE THREE G'S
V. THE THREE W'S

In the 1950s the emerging West Indian Test team produced three extraordinary international cricketers who would probably have walked into any side of their time, or maybe any other time as well.

They became famous in cricketing folklore as a trio but equally famous as individuals. The Three W's – namely Everton Weekes, Frank Worrell and Clyde Walcott were quite simply the outstanding linchpins of the burgeoning West Indian Test side that was to become such a wonderfully dominant force in West Indian cricket in future years.

All three were to be knighted for their services to cricket which of itself is an outstanding recognition of their contribution to international sport. Everton Weekes, born in 1925 played 48 Tests between 1948 and 1958. Frank Worrell, born in 1924 played 51 Tests between 1948 and 1963 and Clyde Walcott born in 1926 played 44 Tests between 1948 and 1960. All three were Barbadians.

Their Test records are:

Worrell: Tests: 51
Inns: 87 No: 9 HS: 261 Runs: 3860 Ave: 49.48
100's: 9 50's: 22 Ct: 43
Balls: 7141 R: 2672 W: 69 Ave: 38.72 BB: 7-70
5W' inns: 2

Weekes: Tests: 48
Inns: 81 No: 5 HS: 207 Runs: 4455 Ave: 58.61 100's: 15
50's: 19 CT: 49
Balls: 122 R: 77 W: 1 Ave: 77.00 BB: 1-8

Walcott: Tests: 44
Inns: 74 No: 7 HS: 220 Runs: 3798 Ave: 56.68 100's: 15
50's: 14 Ct: 53 St: 11
Balls: 1194 R: 408 W: 11 Ave: 37.09 BB: 3-50

It seems quite amazing that three of the finest cricketers ever, were born on a relatively small island within a few miles of each other and within the space of just 18 months.

Combined, these three great players played 143 Tests; they scored over 12,000 runs, 39 centuries, held 145 catches and took 81 wickets. Their combined batting average is 54.81 and bowling average is 38.97. Only Worrell of the three was to captain West Indies (15 times), but he captained neither Weekes nor Walcott, as both had retired from Test cricket.

Frank Worrell was born on 1 August 1924 in Bridgetown, Barbados. He batted right–handed and was perhaps the most stylish and elegant of the three, he bowled left-arm fast medium for most of his career. He was named Wisden cricketer of the year in 1951, was knighted in 1964. He died of leukemia aged just 42.

Clyde Walcott was born on the 17 January 1926 in Bridgetown Barbados. He was a tall powerful right-handed batsman particularly strong off the back foot. For his first 15 Tests he kept wicket until a persistent back injury forced him to give up the gloves but he was also a more than useful fast medium paced swing bowler, he was a Wisden cricketer of the year in 1958 and was knighted in 1994.

Everton Weekes was born on 26 February 1925 in St Michael Bridgetown. A stocky attacking right handed batsman and occasional leg-break bowler he was to set many batting records and was forced through injury to retire too early - in his early thirties. He was knighted in 1995 and was a Wisden cricketer of the year in 1951.

Worrell was to be the first non-white cricketer to captain the West Indies. Weekes and Walcott were to contribute much to cricket after their playing days finished. All three contributed hugely to the game of cricket – not just West Indian cricket.

There have been similar contributions to cricket from for example the Chappell family for Australia, the Pollock family for South Africa, the Hadlee family for New Zealand and, of course, the Grace family for England; but who else for England can compare with the three W's?

Well how about the three G's – Gatting, Gooch and Gower? Like the three W's they all played in the same era, Mike Gatting was born on 6 June 1957 in Kingsbury Middlesex, Graham Gooch on the 23 July in Leytonstone Essex 1953 and David Gower on 1 April 1957 in Tunbridge Wells Kent. The three G's all captained their country with varying degrees of success and at times dominated English cricket

Their records are as follows:

Gatting: Tests: 79
Inns: 138 No: 14 HS: 207 Runs: 4409 Ave: 35.55   100's: 10 50's: 21   Ct:59
Balls: 752 Runs: 317 Wkts: 4 Ave: 79.25 BB:1-14

Gooch: Tests: 118
Inns: 215 No: 6 HS: 333   Runs: 8900 Ave:42.58   100's:20 50's:46   Ct:103
Balls: 2655 Runs:1069 Wkts:23 Ave: 46.48 BB:3-39

Gower: Tests: 117
Inns: 204 No: 18 HS: 215   Runs: 8231 Ave: 44.25   100's: 18 50's:39   Ct:74
Balls:36   Runs: 20 Wkts: 1 Ave: 20.00 BB:1-1

Combined the three G's played 314 Tests - well over double the number played by the three W's, they scored 21,540 runs, scored 48 hundreds, held 236 catches and took just 28 wickets. Their combined batting average is 41.50 and bowling 50.21. On pure statistics alone the three W's win hands down.

Interestingly the three W's played in the same Test side together on 29 occasions whereas the three G's only 27 times, despite playing twice as many Tests between them. There were to be many reasons for this, most notably because of the influence of a nation not even playing Test cricket at the time.

1948
Versus: England

Weekes and Walcott both made their debuts for the West Indies against England in the first test of the tour, in January 1948 at their home Island – Barbados. They were two of a total of seven West Indian debutants. England also capped five new Test players, this is one of highest numbers of debutants in any one Test match.

Walcott was selected to open the batting as well as keep wicket and Weekes to bat at three. The Test was drawn due to torrential rain on the last day with the match well poised with England on 86-2 needing 395 to win. Weekes scored 60 runs in the match; Walcott scored 24 and took 3 catches.

For the next Test in Trinidad Frank Worrell made his debut and so, for the first time, the famous three W's came together in a Test, and batting at four, Worrell scored 97 in his first Test innings; again the match was drawn, but the legend had begun.

It very nearly didn't happen as Weekes was dropped from the original squad, replaced by George Headley, but re-instated when Headley withdrew. England won the toss and batted, Griffith on his debut for England made 140 in his first Test innings. Even more remarkable was that it was his first 'first class' hundred in an England total of 362, the next best score being 55 from Jim Laker batting at number 9 in only his second Test; it was to be the first of only two innings when Laker was to past 50 runs. Laker had made his debut in the first Test in Barbados and had taken 7-103 in the West Indies' first innings including the bowling of Walcott. It was to be Laker's best performance against the West Indies in 13 matches.

Having secured a 135 run first innings lead thanks mainly to a 173 run opening partnership (to match the achievement of Griffith); the West Indian debutant opener Ganteaume in what was to be his only Test innings made 112! The West Indies set about chasing 140 to win and time beat them with their score on 72 for 3. The West Indies changed their batting order for the run chase and promoted Weekes from 3 and Walcott from 5 to open the batting. It was the only time Weekes was to open the batting for the West Indies. Worrell batted again at 4 and top-scored the innings with 28 not out.

All three of the 'W's' played in the remaining two Tests and won them. Walcott, having opened in the first Test, batted at 8 in the fourth.

The third Test was played at Guyana at possibly the only international sports venue (Bourda) to be below sea level - it rained! The West Indies made changes including 2 debutants – Pierre and Trim who opened the bowling and appointed Goddard as captain instead of Gomez who nonetheless kept his place. Goddard promoted himself from number 8 to open and made just 1 and 3. However, his off-break bowling returned Test best figures of 5 for 31 in England's first innings of just 111 and the West Indies won by 7 wickets.

Walcott kept wicket and batted at 3, Worrell at 5 and Weekes having batted at 3 in the previous Test found himself batting at 7. Frank Worrell, in only his third Test innings, made his first Test century – 131 - in a match where the next best score was 63 by England's Hardstaff.

For the fourth and final Test of the series the West Indies again made changes – 3 debutants. Walcott having batted at 2, 3 and 5 now dropped down to number 8 where he made 45 in his only innings. Worrell at 4 made 38 in his only innings and Weekes began his amazing run of five consecutive Test hundreds making 141 as the West Indies won by 10 wickets.

So the three W's legend began. After their first 3 matches playing in the same side together they were unbeaten.

Worrell had scored nearly 300 runs with a top score of 131 not out, Weekes had scored 233 runs with a top score of 141 and Walcott although perhaps disappointing with the bat – 109 runs with a top score of 45 had picked up 8 catches and 5 stumpings.

In the four match series the West Indies won by two Tests to nil. In their careers Worrell lost 17 Tests, won 18 and drew 15 and tied one classic Test. Everton Weekes in his career lost 15 times, won 16 times and drew 17.Walcott lost 13, won 12, and drew 19 Tests.

Worrell in his first Test as West Indies captain playing against Australia in the first Test at Brisbane also played in the first ever tied Test, after over 500 Tests matches had been played.

Batting first the West Indies scored 453 – Worrell 65. Australia replied with 505, Worrell opened the bowling and got through 30 overs – none for 93. In the West Indian second innings Worrell again scored 65 in a total of 284; this was the top score in the innings. Australia needing 233 to win were all out, amidst run outs, chaos and scoring confusion, for 232.

In Australia's second innings Worrell bowled 16 overs in taking 1-41. When playing in their 29 Tests together the three W's lost 12, drew 10, but won only 7. Curiously Worrell's top score of 265 was made against England at Trent Bridge when all three were playing, Walcott made his second best score of 168 not out against England when all three were playing and Weekes' top score of 207 was made against India was when all three were playing.

1948/49
Versus India

Almost as soon as the three greats came together however they split apart. In the winter of 48/49 the West Indies toured India for the first time. There was no Worrell.

There was however no stopping Walcott or particularly Everton Weekes. Having scored his maiden Test hundred in the last Test against England in March, Weekes carried on in India starting with the first Test in November in Delhi, he made scores of 128 – batting at 7 – in the West Indies only innings of a drawn Test followed by 194 batting at 4 in Bombay again in the only West Indies innings of another drawn Test and then 162 and 101 in Calcutta – match drawn. He was dismissed caught and bowled off Ghulam Ahmed in both innings. Five Test centuries in a row, a feat unequalled in Test cricket to date.

Between March 1948 and January 1949 Everton Weekes scored 726 runs in five innings; Hutton for England and Bradman for

Australia were still playing; and they had done battle in the English summer but surely no-one could match this stylish elegant and fearsomely hard hitting West Indian right-hander at this time. The West Indies won the fourth Test in Madras by an innings and Weekes made just 90, he was run out!!!!

The fifth Test back in Bombay was drawn, Weekes scored 56 and 48. In the second innings of the first Test Weekes bowled his first over in Test cricket and in the third Test, as the draw became inevitable Weekes was the tenth bowler used by Goddard.

If Everton Weekes was becoming established as the pre-eminent batsman of his time then Walcott was setting standards as perhaps the first of the genuine all-rounder wicket-keeper batsman. After 15 Tests he was forced to give up the gloves due to a persistent back problem, he was 6ft 2ins tall, tall for a wicket-keeper but, undaunted became a useful fast medium bowler taking 11 Test wickets.

Batting at 4 in the first Test in Delhi he made 152 his maiden hundred, batting at 3 for most of the rest of the series he scored 68, 54, 108, 43, 11 and 16. His 108 was made in just 175 minutes batting at 6 having left the field ill, during his absence his deputy – Christiani picked up a catch and two stumpings. Walcott made 11 dismissals 9 caught and 2 stumped in the series.

Weekes ended the tour with 779 runs at an average of over 111 and Walcott scored over 450 runs at an average of 64.57.

1950
Versus England

In 1950 the West Indies toured England and the three W's reunited. As if that was not enough a certain spin twin combination also toured – Ramadhin and Valentine. England won the first Test at Old Trafford by 202 runs; England wicketkeeper Godfrey Evans batting at 8 made his highest Test score of 104.

Ramadhin and Valentine both made their debuts and took all 10 wickets in England's first innings – Valentine 8-104, Ramadhin bowled 81.3 overs in the match, taking 4-167. Valentine bowled 106 overs in the match finishing with match figures of 11-204.

Walcott had to give up the gloves in England's second innings due to an injury to the West Indies bowler Johnson and he opened the bowling for the West Indies. I can find no other example of a wicket-keeper relinquishing the gloves and then opening the bowling. Perhaps it is not surprising that it was a rare occasion when none of the three great W's succeeded and the West Indies lost. Weekes top scored their first innings with 52.

However, the West Indies won the remaining 3 Tests. In the second Test at Lord's they won by 326 runs – Worrell 97 runs in the match, Weekes 126 runs in the match and Walcott having made 4 dismissals in England's first Innings – including a stumping and a catch each off both Ramadhin and Valentine - made his third Test hundred, his first against England – 168 not out.

The third Test at Trent Bridge was won by the West Indies by a mere 10 wickets. The contribution of the three W's was again significant. Worrell returned 3-40 in England's first innings and then proceeded to make what was to be his best ever Test match score of 261 runs, he shared a fourth wicket partnership of 283 with Everton Weekes who made 129. Walcott contented himself with just 8 runs and 2 dismissals.

In the fourth Test at the Oval the West Indies won by an innings and 56 runs. Batting first the West Indies scored 503 – Worrell batting at three made 138 the highest score of the innings, having retired unwell when his score was 116. He resumed his innings at the fall of the 6th wicket, he did not take the field on the last day as a result of a groin strain. Despite an heroic innings from Sir Len Hutton, who carried his bat for 202 in England's first innings (a feat never before achieved against the West Indies); England following on collapsed to 103 in their second innings, Weekes held three catches.

At the end of 1950 the three W's had played seven times together all versus England. They had won 5 lost 1 and drawn 1. Weekes had scored 571 runs at 57.10, Walcott 338 runs plus 20 dismissals and Worrell had scored 833 runs and taken 7 wickets.

After the end of this four test series West Indies had completed a 3 – 1 series win. In the series Worrell had scored 539 runs at 89.83 and taken 6 wickets at 30.33. Weekes had averaged over 56 runs per innings and Walcott had made 7 dismissals and averaged over 45.

1951-52
Versus Australia

For the first time the three W's toured Australia together. It was only the second time the West Indies had toured Australia and only the second series between the two countries. For Australia; Lindwall and Miller were playing, Benaud debuted in the second Test and Australia where captained by Hassett. The West Indies lost the series 4-1. It was a hard time for the West Indies but the three W's battled hard for their country, playing together in only three of the five Tests.

The first Test at Brisbane was to be a close game. Worrell batting at three came in with the West Indies having lost their first wicket for naught in a West Indies total of 216, he was the second top scorer with 37. Weekes came close with 35 and Walcott made what was remarkably to be the only duck of his Test career of 74 innings - LBW to Lindwall. Australia won by 3 wickets. Weekes top scored in the West Indies second innings with 70. In a low scoring match he was the only player to aggregate over 100 runs in the Test.

In the second Test at Sydney Australia won by 7 wickets. Batting first the West Indies made 362 runs, Worrell 64, Walcott 60 and Weekes but 5; in a second innings total of 290 Walcott was the second highest scorer with 56 and took 2 catches and made a stumping. Worrell took 2 wickets for 67 runs in the match. It was the first time the three had suffered back to back defeats.

In a rain affected third Test Walcott did not play but the West Indies won by 6 wickets. Batting first Australia were dismissed for just 82, Worrell bowled unchanged and took 6 for 38. The West Indies replied with just 105 all out but Weekes was their top scorer with 26. Valentine took 6 wickets in the Australian second innings and the West Indies won.

The fourth Test at Melbourne was a thriller and was won by Australia by just one wicket. Australia's last wicket pair of Ring and Johnston scoring 38 runs to win the Test. Perhaps this of all Tests proved the worth of Worrell, batting at 3 with a badly bruised hand he made 108 in their first innings – the next best score was 37. Worrell's injury restricted him to bowling just 9 overs in the second innings of the match (1-18) and maybe it would have been a different result if he had been fully fit. Weekes made scores of 1 and 2.

For the final Test of the tour Walcott returned to the side and for the first time as a specialist batsman. As a result of his nagging back problems he was never to keep wicket again. It is noteworthy that for the rest of his Test career the West Indies tried seven different wicket keepers, chopping and changing often, including using 3 different 'keepers in one series, undeterred Walcott was to become a very useful medium pace swing bowler.

Australia won by 202 runs. In a bizarre first day on a good wicket in hot weather 19 wickets fell for just 180 runs. The West Indies bowled Australia out for 116 – Worrell 3-42 but were then dismissed themselves for just 78. It was one of the few times that all of the three W's failed to reach double figures when playing together; Walcott 1, Worrell 6 and Weekes 0 – the first duck of his Test career.

The three had played in three of the 5 Tests and had lost them all and lost the series 4-1. In a beaten side Worrell proved what a fine all-rounder he was with a batting average of 33.70 and 17 wickets at 19.35, Weekes averaged just 24.50 in 10 innings with a top score of 70 and Walcott averaged just 14.50 from 6 innings with a top score of 60.

The West Indies then moved for a 2 Test series against New Zealand, the first time the two nations had played Test cricket. The 3 W's played both Tests. They won the first Test at Christchurch by 5 wickets and drew the second in Auckland.

In the first Test Worrell batting at 3 made 71 and 62 not out and opened the bowling none for 25 off 11 overs, Walcott made 65 and 19 but Weekes just 7 and 2. The second Test was rain affected but batting first the West Indies scored 546 for 6 declared. Weekes batted at 4 and made 51 and Worrell batting at 5 with Walcott at 6 put on 189 for the fifth wicket, Worrell made exactly 100 and Walcott 115. It was to be one of their most successful Tests together.

Having conceded only just over two runs per over in the first innings, Worrell bowled 15 overs, 6 maidens, taking 1 wicket for just 24 runs in New Zealand's second innings.

1952-53
Versus India

The now firmly established trio played all 5 Tests in the West Indies against India. The West Indies won the series 1-0; winning the second Test at Barbados by 142 runs, the other four Tests being drawn. Matting wickets were being used and in the first Test, Weekes made 207, it was to be his Test best, Walcott made 47 and in India's second innings Worrell bowled 20 overs 2-32 and Walcott bowled 16 overs of which 10 were maidens and took 2 wickets for 12 - his first wickets in Tests.

In their first innings Weekes made 47 and Walcott 98. The third Test was played in Trinidad, it was scheduled for Georgetown but it was flooded. In the first innings total of 315 Weekes scored 161 run out it was his sixth hundred in eight Tests against India in the second innings he was 55 not out.

Worrell bowled 57 overs in the match taking 4-109. With the game over as a contest Weekes' occasional leg spin was used for the first time in Tests, one over for one run.

The fourth Test at Bourda was ruined by rain but the three W's all scored runs – Worrell batting at number 3 scored 56, Weekes at 4 made 86 and Walcott, batting at 5 and in his 13th innings in the West Indies scored his first hundred in a home match – 125.

The fifth Test in Jamaica saw the West Indies chasing 181 to win in only some 2 half hours in their second innings, the West Indies were at one stage 15 for 2 and already holding a 1-0 lead in the series they settled for a draw.

In their first innings, however, the 3 W's set a new first; all three passed 100 runs in the same innings: Worrell, batting at 3 made 237, Weekes batting at 4 made 109; they put on 197 runs for the West Indies third wicket and with Walcott, Worrell added 213 for the fourth wicket, with Walcott following his century in the previous Test scoring 118 in a total of 576. In India's second innings, Weekes held 4 catches.

At the end of this series the three W's had played together seventeen times. They had only lost four times, three against Australia and once against England. Worrell had scored over 1,600 runs at 67.88 with 6 fifties and 5 hundreds and had taken 26 wickets at 35.58.

Weekes had scored over 1,500 runs at 59.00 with 8 fifties and 5 hundreds, and Walcott had made just short of a 1,000 runs at an average of over 43, he had taken 23 catches (9 as a fielder) and 11stumpings. He had also taken 2 wickets both against India.

1953-54
Versus England

Having played together in ten of the last twelve Tests and seven times against England, the trio did not play together in this series against England until the third match of the series. Worrell missed the first and Weekes the second, the West Indies had won both comfortably.

In the second Test in Barbados, his birthplace, Walcott batting at 4, scored 220 in the West Indies first innings. It was to be his highest score in Tests.

Ironically with the three back together for the third Test in Guyana they lost. Len Hutton made 169 in England's first innings, Weekes top scored for the West Indies scoring 94, and Worrell had perhaps one of his least successful matches. He opened the batting in the first innings and made a rare duck, the first of Statham's six wickets in the match and made only two in his second knock batting at 3. He also opened the bowling and was wicket-less. Walcott made just 30 runs in the match.

The fourth Test was played on a matting wicket in Trinidad and the batsmen flourished – over 1500 runs were scored and only 24 wickets fell. Four England bowlers conceded over 100 runs in the first innings and the three W's returned to form with a vengeance.

For the second time when playing together all 3 W's scored over 100: Weekes at 3 made 206, Worrell at 4 made 167 and Walcott at 5 scored 124. For the third wicket Weekes and Worrell put a record partnership of 338. By the end of the match the West Indies had used 10 bowlers. Weekes bowled 5 overs in the second innings and Walcott in the first innings bowled 34 overs taking 3 for 52, the best analysis in the match.

The fifth Test was played at Jamaica and saw the England comeback complete. They won by 9 wickets to square the series. It was the first time the West Indies had lost at Sabina Park. Hutton made 205 and Trevor Bailey took 7-34. Two of the 3 W's had a poor time, Weekes made 0 and 3, Worrell 4 and 29.

In the first innings the West Indies who had won the toss and batted were at one stage were 13 for 4. Walcott however battled bravely, he top scored the first innings with 50 and also the second innings with his ninth hundred – 116. He also took the prize wicket of Hutton - when he was on 205!

This was not the worst wicket to take as Hutton finished the series with over 670 runs in only eight innings and for only seven times out. The series was therefore squared two matches each.

Worrell had scored 334 runs at 47.71 but taken only 2 wickets at 96.00. Walcott had scored nearly 700 runs and taken 4 wickets and Weekes had scored 487 runs in four Tests including a double hundred, averaging 69.57.

1954-55
Versus Australia

Australia came to the West Indies with amongst others; Lindwall, Miller, Benaud and Harvey in their side. Australia won the series 3 Tests to nil with 2 drawn.

This was perhaps the series of the batsman, in the five Tests a total of 6198 runs were scored and only 149 wickets were taken. Twenty one centuries were scored and of the nine scored by the West Indies Walcott made five of them. The 3 W's played four of the five Tests (Worrell missed the second test). The first Test was a comfortable 9 wicket win for Australia, Harvey 133 and Miller 147 were both dismissed by Walcott, he added Benaud to his victims in returning his Test best of 3-50 and then top scored with 108 in the West Indies first innings total of 259.

With Australia needing but 20 to win Weekes bowled and took his only Test wicket Arthur Morris caught by Gibbs for 1. Arthur Morris was a fine and dogged opening bat for Australia, he played 46 times for Australia, scored over 3,500 runs at an average of over 46. I suspect this was perhaps the one dismissal he would most want to forget.

No Worrell for the second Test but Weekes and Walcott put on a record 242 for the third wicket – Walcott 126, Weekes 139. Walcott with 110 in the second innings joined Weekes as one of only three West Indians at that time to have scored hundreds in both innings of a Test. The match was drawn with Australia making exacting 600 for 9 declared in their only innings, a rare occasion when all three of Australia's top three made hundreds – Macdonald 110, Morris 111 and Harvey 133.

Worrell was back for the third Test – Australia won by 8 wickets. All 3 W's made contributions, Weekes made 81 in the West Indians first innings, it was the top score. The next best score was 16, he then made a rare duck in his second innings. Walcott made 73 in the second innings again the top score and was dismissed in one of the rarer ways – hit wicket, bowled Lindwall. Bizarrely Worrell, having made 51 in the second innings, was also dismissed hit wicket, he fell to Benaud.

The fourth Test was played at the home of the 3 W's – Barbados, 1,661 runs were scored in the match. In Australia's first innings total of 668 all out, four players passed 50 and 2 – Miller and Lindwall made hundreds. Worrell bowled 40 overs taking 2-120 and only Walcott of the 3 W's with 83 in the second innings passed 50 runs. Walcott was perhaps at his best in this series. The final Test was played in Jamaica and the Australians won by an innings.

The West Indies won the toss and batted, they made 357, Walcott at 3 scored 155, Weekes 56 and Worrell 61. The Australians, however, replied with one of the highest Test scores ever – 758 for 8 declared with five centurions: Mcdonald 127, Harvey 204, Miller 109, Archer 128 and Benaud 121 (in just 78 minutes). This was the first time in the history of Test cricket that five hundreds had been scored in the same innings.

Worrell having bowled 40 overs at Barbados now bowled 45 overs taking 1-116 in Australia's only innings. The West Indies used 6 bowlers and 5 conceded over 100 runs – another first in the history of Test cricket. The sixth bowler was Gary Sobers and he went for 99 runs in 38 overs!

In their second innings Walcott produced a unique double, for the second time he made a hundred in both innings of a Test in the same series – 110 to follow his 155 in the West Indies first innings. Weekes was injured and had to bat at 9 he was 36 not out. Walcott finished the series having played four Tests with 827 runs, 5 hundreds, 2 fifties and an average of 82.70. He also held 3 catches and produced his Test best bowling of 3-50. Worrell scored just 206 runs at an average of 25.75 and a top score of 61 and took just 3 wickets. Weekes made 469 runs including one hundred and three 50's. He averaged 58.62.

1955-56
Versus New Zealand
The beginning of the end

The era of the 3 W's was drawing to an end. In 1955-56 the West Indies toured New Zealand for a four Test series. Only Weekes of the 3 W's featured. The West Indies won easily by 3 Tests to one. They won the first and second Tests by an innings and the third by 9 wickets.

Weekes scored: 123, 103, 156, three consecutive hundreds in the first three Tests and in defeat in the fourth Test he scored just 5 and 31, he averaged 85 and also held five catches. Ramadhin, 20 wickets in the series and Valentine, 15 wickets were spinning their magic, Sir Garfield Sobers was becoming seen as a premier all-rounder and Weekes, the most experienced and longest serving member of the side captained by Atkinson led by example.

After Weekes' three hundreds the next highest score by a West Indian was 83. The highest score by a New Zealander in the entire series was 84.

1957
Versus England
The Last Hurrah

In 1957 the 3 W's toured England together and played together for the last time. They were to play all five Tests. England won the series three Tests to nil.

Some of the most famous and iconic England cricketers played in this series: May, Cowdrey, Laker and Lock, Trueman and Statham, Graveney, Close and Sheppard. But so did several West Indians; apart from the three W's, the West Indians had Sobers, Kanhai, Ramadhin and Valentine in their squad.

The first Test at Birmingham was drawn, England were dismissed in their first innings for just 186 having chosen to bat first. Ramadhin 7-48.

The West Indies replied with 474, Walcott at 3 made 90 Worrell low down at 8 made 81, Weekes failed scoring just 9. The West Indies therefore securing a first innings lead of 288 runs.

This was the Test of the famous, perhaps infamous May, Cowdrey partnership of 411 in England's second innings total of 583 for 4 declared England captain Peter May made 285 not out which was to be his highest Test score, and Cowdrey scored 154. It was the first time in 28 years that England had staged a Test at Edgbaston. Ramadhin wheeled away for 98 overs more than ever bowled in an innings taking 2-179, Valentine did not play. In their second innings the stuffing had been kicked out of the West Indians. Walcott made 1, Worrell naught and Weekes the top score of the innings made 33 as the match ended with a demoralised West Indian side 72 for 7, chasing 295 to win.

A rare event for England in that the second Test was played at Lord's and England won - by an innings. Walcott batted at 3 and made 14 and 21 out to Trevor Bailey both times, Weekes was also a Bailey victim both times but in the second innings again top scored for the West Indies with 90. Worrell scored just 22 runs also out to Bailey in the first innings but bowled 42 overs taking 2-114. He had a smidgen of revenge in that he bowled Bailey for 1.

The third Test at Trent Bridge was drawn and Worrell promoted to open the batting achieved one of the rarest and most notable events in cricket; replying to a massive England total of 619 for 6 declared – May, following his historic 285 had scored 104, Worrell 'carried his bat' for 191 not out.

The next best score was by his opening partner Sobers who made 47. Worrell had also opened the bowling and got through 21 overs (1-79). Weekes made 33 and Walcott 17. In their second innings Worrell made 16, Weekes 3 and Walcott 7. England won the fourth Test at Headingley by an innings. Weekes made 0 and 14, Walcott 38 and 35 and Worrell opening made 29 and 7.

However, with the powers of Weekes and Walcott perhaps starting to fail, Worrell having carried his bat at Trent Bridge now produced his best ever bowling analysis of 7-70 opening the bowling.

And so to the Oval in August 1957, the three W's played together for the last time. It was to be a slightly sad end to their three careers as one. England won by an innings and 237 runs. England scored 412 – Graveney 164 and then dismissed the West Indies for two of their lowest scores ever – 89 and 86. Lock and Laker held sway for England; I cannot find any record of a calypso about these two but perhaps there should be: Lock took 11-48 and Laker 5-77 in the match.

Weekes, for the only time in his career made a pair: caught by Trueman off Laker 0 in the first innings and bowled by Lock for 0 in the second innings, Worrell, opening the batting was also out to Lock in the second innings for naught having made 4 in the first innings. And Walcott made just 5 and 19.

The three W's had first played together in Trinidad against England in 1948 they had scored over 200 runs, in 1958 at the Oval they made just 28.

Their Test careers, having started at almost the same time, were to end in a much more varied fashion. Everton Weekes played his last Test against Pakistan in Trinidad in March 1958, Pakistan won by an innings. Weekes made 51 in the first innings and Walcott, at number: 5 scored 47 and 62. Weekes bowled 3 overs for 4 runs. Worrell did not play. Weekes was only 33 years old but a series of niggling injuries, including a persistent thigh problem persuaded him to give up playing Test cricket.

He continued to play for Barbados and played for Bacup in the Lancashire league. Following retirement he coached in Barbados and served as an ICC match referee. Having already been awarded an MBE and CBE he was knighted in 1995.

In a first class career of 152 matches Weekes scored over 12,000 runs at 55.34 with 36 centuries but in an oft used litmus Test of a truly fine player it is notable that his Test batting average was even better: 58.61.

Walcott played his last Test against England in the fifth and final Test at Trinidad in March 1960. He made 53 in their first innings and, in a drawn match, he also bowled 4 overs. He retired from Test cricket aged just 34. It has been debated as to whether this was because of his frustration with the 'island-centric' politics of West Indian Cricket at the time or simply over pay. Walcott himself is attributed with claiming it was over the latter.

He played for both Barbados and Guyana as well as Enfield in the Lancashire League. He became a respected coach and managed three West Indian touring teams including the World Cup winning side of 1975. He was an ICC match referee and chairman of the ICC. He was a Wisden Cricketer of the year 1958 and knighted in 1994.

Worrell was to play for another three years, making his last appearance for the West Indies in the last Test of their 1963 tour of England at the Oval. He was the captain of the side. The West Indies won the Test by 8 wickets giving them an historic 3-1 series victory in England. Batting at 7 he made just 9 runs and bowled just 5 overs without success.

It could be said that Worrell contributed hugely to uniting the geographically and politically split countries that made up the West Indies into one powerful proud and successful cricketing side. He too played Lancashire League cricket for Radcliffe, he took an economics degree at Manchester University and married his wife Velda in Radcliffe. For the first time a cricketer was honored with a memorial service at Westminster Abbey.

A strong, proud and immensely talented cricketer he was knighted in 1964.

The three W's in 242 innings failed to score on just eighteen occasions; of which 12 ducks were against England. Walcott failed to score only once in his entire Test career.

They seemed to like playing against England; Weekes and Worrell scored 338 for the third wicket against England at Port-of-Spain in 1954 and Worrell's highest score 261 was made at Trent Bridge in 1950. Weekes' 206 in 1953/54 in Trinidad was his second best in Tests by just one run, having made 207 against India and Worrell's 216 again at Trent Bridge in 1950 also his Test best. Their individual records against England make interesting reading:

Against England:

Worrell: Tests: 25 W: 9 L: 8 D: 8
Inns: 41 No: 6 HS: 261 Runs: 1979 Ave: 56.54
100's: 6 50's: 7 Ct: 18
Balls: 3159 Runs:1211 Wkts: 28 BB: 7-70 Ave: 43.25

Weekes: Tests: 17 W: 6 L: 6 D: 5
Inns: 30 No: 1 HS: 206 Runs: 1251 Ave: 43.14
100's: 3 50's: 6 Ct: 16
Balls: 42 Runs: 42 Wkts: 0 BB: 0-3 Ave: -

Walcott: Tests: 20 W: 7 L: 6 D: 7
Inns: 36 No: 5 HS: 220 Runs: 1391 Ave: 44.87
100's: 4 50's: 5 Ct: 24 St: 8
Balls: 468 Runs: 180 Wkts: 5 BB: 3-52 Ave: 36.00

Interestingly, despite playing many more Tests in admittedly a far busier time of Test cricket, the 3 G's probably did not enjoy their Tests against the West Indies to quite the same extent as the 3W's did when playing against England in fact Gooch, Gower and Gatting as a trio played less Tests against the West Indies than the 3 W's played against England.

Their records against admittedly awesomely strong West Indies sides, and in a totally different era and playing many more Tests against more Test playing countries make for astonishing and depressing reading.

Neither Gower nor Gatting were ever to be on the winning side against the West Indies and Gooch was to be on the winning side just three times in 26 Tests. Gooch's individual record against the West Indies is however outstanding and worthy of high praise given the various circumstances and pressures in which he played.

The record of Gower by no means suffers that badly in comparison either. Gatting however, and his nose, might wish that his record against the West Indies could be expunged.

Against the West Indies:

Gooch: Tests: 26 W: 3 L: 14 D: 9
Inns: 51 No: 2 HS: 154* Runs: 2197 Ave: 44.84
100's: 5 50's: 13 Ct: 28
Balls: 324 Runs: 136 Wkts: 4 BB: 2-18 Ave: 34.00

Gower: Tests: 19 W: 0 L: 16 D: 3
Inns: 38 No: 3 HS: 154* Runs: 1149 Ave: 32.83
100's: 1 50's: 6 Ct: 11
Did not bowl.

Gatting: Tests: 9 W: 0 L: 4 D: 5
Inns: 17 No: 0 HS: 56 Runs: 258 Ave: 15.12
100's: 0 50's: 1 Ct: 7
Did not bowl.

In their respective Test careers Gooch made 13 ducks in 215 innings (3 against the West Indies in 51 innings), Gower made just 7 ducks in 204 innings (none against the West Indies) and Gatting 16 ducks in 138 innings of which 2 were against the West Indies.

PART II
The 3 G's

So how do the 'three G's' compare to the 'three W's'?

It must be said that their records do not in any way match those of the three W's but maybe their commitment and influence on English cricket is equally dominant in the era in which they played.

GOOCH

Graham Gooch was the first of the three G's to play for England. He was born on the 23 July 1953 in Leytonstone, Essex. He made his Essex debut in 1973, was capped by them in 1975 and was a Wisden cricketer of the year in 1980. A right-handed bat, excellent slip fielder and right-arm medium bowler who perhaps could and should have bowled a little more, he was a fearless and strong striker of a cricket ball, equally strong driving off the front foot and cutting or pulling off the back foot. He was a somewhat enigmatic and private person, determined and dedicated; a committed West Ham supporter he was known at times to train with their footballers. He tried to bring the same level of fitness and team-ness to England, with mixed fortunes. I feel he was something of a reluctant captain, if only because of his rather prickly relationship with the British media; partly perhaps brought on by himself. Never totally comfortable with the media, he has now however become a more than capable commentator, having also served as an England selector. He captained his county 1986-87 and again from 1989 to 1994 he played for Essex until retiring in 1997. In his first class career he scored over 44,800 runs at an average of 49.01, scoring 128 hundreds and 217 fifties held 555 catches and took 246 wickets at 34.37 with a best of 7-14, making him one of the most prolific run-makers in the English game.

Gooch was to play 118 Tests for England and 125 one day internationals. He was to captain England in 34 Tests and 49 one day internationals.

His record as England Test captain is:

```
        Pl  W   L   D
Tests:  34  10  12  12
```
Inns: 63 No: 2 HS: 333 Runs: 3582 Ave: 58.72
100's: 11 50's: 16
Balls: 828 Runs: 338 Wkts: 8 BB: 3-39 Ave: 42.25

His overall Test and one day record is:

Tests: 118 W: 32 L: 42 D: 44
Inns: 215 No: 6 HS: 333 Runs: 8900 Ave: 42.58
100's: 20 50's: 46 Ct: 103
Balls: 2655 Runs:1069 Wkts: 23 BB: 3-39 Ave: 46.47

ODI's 125: W: 64 L: 56 Tied: 1 No result: 4
Inns: 122 No: 6 HS: 142 Runs: 4290 Ave: 36.98
100's: 8 50's: 23
Balls: 2066 Runs:1516 Wkts:36 BB: 3-19 Ave: 42.11

In his Test career he was to become the highest ever aggregate run scorer for his country to date, scoring 8,900 runs at an average of 42.58 with 46 fifties and 20 hundreds with a highest score of 333 at Lord's against India in 1990. He held 103 catches, a record for England to date and took 23 Test wickets at an average of 46.47.

In one day internationals he finished with an average of 36.98 in 125 matches with a highest score of 142.

GATTING

Michael Gatting was born on 6 June 1957 in Kingsbury, Middlesex. He made his Middlesex debut in 1975, and was capped by his county in 1977, he captained Middlesex from 1983-1997.

A belligerent, squat, strutting, bearded right-handed batsman, Mike Gatting was a famous and instantly recognisable player. Uncompromising and hard-hitting he was at his best driving, often with fearsome venom off the front foot through the off-side. Despite the good humoured – for most of the time – jokes about his stocky, even tubby size Gatting was a terrific player of spin bowling, quick of eye and foot. Of the three G's he was to have the most difficult, stop-start international career. Like his two 'G's' colleagues he too was to captain his country.

He was also I believe a somewhat reluctant captain of his country, and his captaincy was also to include highs and lows and controversy, perhaps more so than either those of Gooch or Gower. A tough straightforward man, who perhaps had a little too much faith in the basic decency and honesty of his fellow man, he was undone by allegations of cheating and tabloid media sensationalism, added to an insensitive handling of his situation and, perhaps in a fit of two fingered pique, even temper, he went on an ill-judged tour to South Africa.

This decision was made, I feel, as his only answer to the authorities whom he may have felt had not played fair by him. He was to play 79 Tests for England, 23 as captain, and 92 One Day Internationals, 37 as captain.

His Test average was 35.55, scoring 4409 runs including 10 100's and 21 fifties. He held 59 Test catches and also took 4 wickets in bowling 752 balls at an average of 79.25.

Gatting's international career as captain is as follows:

Tests 23 W: 2 L: 5 D: 16
Inns: 39 No: 4 HS: 183* Runs: 1542 Ave: 44.05
100's: 5 50's: 5
Balls: 420 Runs: 150 Wkts: 2 BB: 1-21 Ave: 75.00

ODI's: 37 W: 26 L: 11 D: 0
Inns: 37 No: 7 HS: 82 Runs: 1013 Ave: 33.76
100's: 0 50's: 5
Balls: 138 Runs: 122 Wkts: 4 BB: 3-59 Ave: 30.50

Gatting's overall test and one day record is:

Tests: 79 W: 15 L: 26 D: 38
Inns: 138 No: 14 HS: 207 Runs: 4409 Ave:35.55
100's: 10 50's: 21 Ct: 59
Balls: 752 Runs: 317 Wkts: 4 BB: 1-14 Ave: 79.25

ODI's: 92 W: 54 L: 37 No result: 0 Tied: 1
Inns: 88 No: 17 HS:115* Runs: 2095 Ave: 29.50
100's: 1 50's: 9
Balls: 392 Runs: 336 Wkts: 10 BB: 3-32 Ave: 33.60

GOWER

David Gower was perhaps the most naturally gifted of the three, he was born on 1 April 1957 in Tunbridge Wells, Kent. Perhaps a fitting date for such a wonderfully and naturally gifted and at times, frustrating player.

He made his county debut for Leicestershire in 1975, was capped by his County in 1977, was a Wisden cricketer of the year in 1978 and Captained Leicestershire from 1984-86. In 1990 he moved to Hampshire where he played out his county career until a perhaps premature retirement in 1993; when he moved as effortlessly as any of his strokes to the commentary box.

He averaged over 40 in first class cricket; scoring 26,339 runs with 53 100's and 136 50's. He was to play 117 Tests for England, 32 of them as captain and 114 one day internationals – 24 as captain. He scored 8,231 Test runs with 18 hundreds, 39 fifties and an average of 44.25 and also scored 3170 one-day runs at an average of 30.77. It may be that it says all about Gower to note that his Test average exceeds his overall first class average. David Gower can only be described as an elegant left-handed batsman whose greatest asset and most frustrating trait was his sheer instinctive ability. He was a very occasional right-arm off-break bowler. I truly believe that Gower played his cricket almost totally by instinct based on a natural ability. He had an innate ability to thrill and infuriate almost in the one shot and certainly in the one innings. He was always, from his very first ball in Test cricket (flicked effortlessly to the fine-leg boundary for four) and for the whole of his international career to play in the same style – the margin between success and failure in any international sport is infinitesimal and Gower epitomised this. He was perhaps at one and the same time both a victim and a hero of his natural talent. He could play exactly the same shot to two seemingly identical deliveries; one would almost caress or whisper its way to the boundary, one would nick to slip.

The crowd, the press and his team-mates would sigh and so, inwardly would the man himself, but few would realise it.
So often the scribes and experts would opine that 'Gower is struggling to find his form'.
Rubbish! With Gower it was rarely, if ever a case of being in or out of form. He simply played the same way ball by ball, over by over, innings by innings and match by match. Confidence may on very rare occasions have been an issue; but never form. He too was to captain his country and to feel the pressure of bad management and the perception that he was too unconcerned and too laissez-faire. He genuinely believed that all England cricketers could and should be allowed to trust to their abilities and largely be left to get on with their game. He was undoubtedly the cheese to Gooch's chalk and the two were never to be truly confident in each other. Their whole attitude and ethos was so different, he was the only one of the three to have two separate spells as captain.

Gower's record as captain is:
Tests: 32 W: 5 L: 18 D: 9
Inns: 55 No: 3 HS: 215 Runs: 2267 Ave: 43.59
100's: 6 50's: 9
Balls: 18 Runs: 13 Wkts: 0

ODI's: 24 W: 10 L: 13 No result: 0 Tied: 1
Inns: 24 No: 0 Runs: 601 HS: 102 Ave: 25.04
100's: 1 50's: 2
Balls: 2 Runs: 9 Wkts: 0

Gower's overall test and one day record is:
Tests: 117 W: 32 L: 42 D: 43
Inns: 204 No: 18 HS: 215 Runs: 8231 Ave: 44.25 100's: 18 50's: 39 Ct: 74
Balls: 36 Runs: 20 Wkts: 1 BB: 1-1 Ave: 20.00

ODI's: 114
Inns: 111 No: 8 HS: 158 Runs: 3170 Ave: 30.77

100's: 7 50's: 12 Ct: 44
Balls: 5 Runs:14 Wkts: 0

Batting Order(s)

In the same way as the three W's were to bat in several different positions in the batting order, so were the three G's.

In his 48 Tests Weekes batted at No. 4 for most his career, 57 of his 81 innings, but batted at 3 or 5 nine times, at 7 or 6 twice and once at number 9. Worrell in 51 Tests and 87 innings batted in almost every position in the order: he batted at number1 six times, at 3 twenty three times, at 4 twelve times at 5 twenty one times, at 6 eight times, 7 thirteen times, 8 three times and once at number 9. Walcott 44 Tests, 74 innings batted at number 2 three times, at 3 twenty three times, at 4 eight times at 5 thirty one times at 6 seven times and twice he batted as low as number 8.

Gooch in 118 Tests and 218 innings was to bat at either 1 or 2 in almost all of his Tests, he batted at 5 in thirteen innings, at 4 ten times and at number 3 eight times; Gower in 117 Tests and over 200 innings batted for the majority of his career at either 4 or 5 but even he opened the batting for England twice, in the second innings against India at Kanpur in a drawn Test and again in a second innings this time at Trent Bridge against Australia, on both occasions he was captain and he batted at 3 seventeen times and also at 6 three times and number 7 twice.

Gatting in 79 Tests equally batted in several places in the England order. The majority of his Test innings were either at 4 or 5, but he batted on thirty seven occasions in what was at the time a troublesome position for England of number 3, and in two Tests on the tour of Pakistan in 1983-84 he had to open the batting.

Gooch was, for me, a most reassuring figure as an opener, but in my opinion neither Gower nor Gatting should have ever batted higher than four or three at a push.

The concept and playing of One Day internationals was of course not present during the careers of the three W's but I wonder just how they would have performed in this format of the game? I suspect that Walcott would have walked into any side as a batman wicket-keeper and later in his career a more than useful bowler, Worrell as a genuine and outstanding all-rounder would have been a strong candidate, and Weekes as a potential match winning batsman would also have had to have been included.

I suspect that in almost any one-day international squad of sixteen players in the modern era all three would have a very strong case for inclusion.

1975
Versus Australia
Gooch Debut

So to careers of the 3 G's

In 1974 Graham Gooch scored 637 runs for Essex at an average of 28.95 with 1 hundred and 2 fifties. England were playing Australia in 1975 and Gooch was selected for the first Test of the series at Edgbaston in July; he was 21 years old.

The Australian side included two Chappells, Ian and Greg, Rodney Marsh and a couple of useful pace bowlers in Lillee and Thomson. The England side was to be captained for the last time by Mike Denness.

In the previous winter England had toured Australia and had, quite simply, been murdered. The result of the most famous of all international sporting trophies was that they – the Ashes - had been regained by Australia by a margin of 4 Tests to 0.

Lillee and Thomson were the most fearsome and potent of fast bowling attacks. In the first Test alone they fractured the hands of two of England's finest openers, Amiss and Edrich. Thomson finished the series with 33 wickets and Lillee took 25 wickets.

England had quite simply been battered and beaten into submission to the extent that the captain Denness dropped himself for the fourth Test having scored just 65 runs in 6 innings and that Colin Cowdrey – later Lord Cowdrey – was by common request of the battered and beleaguered side flown out for his sixth tour to Australia, to bolster the batting.

Cowdrey at the age of 42, just a few days short of his 43rd birthday, and not having played for his country since 1971 joined the tour, he played in the second Test at Perth – then acknowledged as one of the truest but fasted pitches in the world against two of the fastest bowlers of their time just four days after arriving in Australia.

So 1975 for Graham Gooch may not have been the best time to make a debut and not the easiest of sides against which to debut.

For this first Test of the summer Denness retained the captaincy and, on winning the toss, inserted the Aussies! He had perhaps not looked closely enough at the weather forecast. Australia made 359- Marsh topped scored with 61 and John Snow took 3-86 for England.

The heavens opened, England got trapped on a wet wicket in overcast conditions and lost by an innings and 85 runs. Lillee took 7 wickets in the match and Thomson 5. Denness lost the captaincy and was never to play for England again. Graham Gooch batting at 5 was to join the company of many other England players on debut, he made 'a pair', - caught Marsh, bowled Walker in the first innings after only three deliveries and caught Marsh bowled Thomson in the second innings when he faced just 7 deliveries. For a man who was to become England's leading run scorer this was not an auspicious start.

Tony Greig took the captaincy for the second Test at Lord's. David Steele, who was to briefly become a most unlikely sporting icon and win the BBC Sports Personality of the year, and Bob Woolmer made England debuts. Gooch retained his place at five and scored 6 and 31 in a drawn Test. He was dropped for the remainder of the series!

Graham Gooch, highly regarded, and hopeful returned to Essex a chastened man. It was to be three years and some 24 Tests before Gooch was to see the inside of an England dressing room again.

1977/78
Versus Pakistan.
Gatting Debut

Mike Gatting now made his England debut in the third Test against Pakistan at Karachi when neither Gooch nor Gower where present.

In 1977 Gatting had scored 1,095 runs for Middlesex at an average of 33.18. He was 21 years old when selected for the winter tours – being 3 Tests versus Pakistan followed by 3 against New Zealand. All three Tests in Pakistan were boring draws with appallingly slow scoring. In the first Test at Lahore Mudassar Nazar scored the slowest Test hundred recorded – 557 minutes, Boycott joined in by taking 290 minutes over 50.

In a one day match Brearley had his arm broken by Sikander Bakht and Boycott took over the captaincy of England for the first time and in his 69th Test match. So Gatting, in a portend of things to come made his debut and played against Pakistan in the third Test in Karachi and, batting at 5, he was dismissed LBW in both innings in scoring just 5 and 6. He was one of 6 LBW decisions in England's first innings, this was a record at the time. England claimed 4 LBW decisions and Pakistan 9 in the three Test series. Gatting was struggling on the tour to get established as an England player – having scored just 11 runs in Pakistan he was selected for the third and final Test in Auckland and made 5 in England's first innings, the match was drawn and he did not bat in the second innings. In his first two Tests in 3 innings Gatting had scored 11 runs.

1977/78
Versus New Zealand

England performed abysmally in the first Test against New Zealand in Wellington in February 1978. They lost against New Zealand for the first time ever and recorded one of their lowest scores ever – 64 all out in their second innings. England managed to bounce back in the second Test winning by 174 runs. For the third and deciding Test Rose was dropped, Randall promoted to open the innings and Gatting was recalled and, in England's only innings of 315, in a drawn match Gatting made naught. Gatting like Gooch, had made an inauspicious start to his Test career and, like Gooch was to wait several Tests before being given another chance.

World Series cricket had come along and all of cricket was trying both on and off the field to come to terms with the cricketing, financial and legal ramifications of Mr.Packer's so called Circus. Several very good, high profile and successful cricketers had hitched their wagon to World Series cricket and the whole international game was in a state of legal and moral confusion.

Gatting, despite this, was to have to wait until 1980 and twenty Tests for another England chance.

1978
Versus Pakistan
Gower debut

In the first Test of the summer of 1978 David Gower made his Test debut in the first Test at Edgbaston against Pakistan flicking his first ball in Test cricket off Liaquat Ali for a sumptuous four to fine leg and going on to make 58 in England's only innings. England won by an innings and 57 runs. In 1977 the languid somewhat laissez-faire left-handed batsman had made 748 for Leicestershire at 23.28 and in 1978 was to pass 1,000 runs at 37.86. So to the second Test when for the first time two of the three G's appeared together in an England team. Gooch replaced

Barry Wood the Lancashire left-hander for the second Test and, opening with Brearley, he made 54 in an England total of 364. David Gower, taking to Test cricket like the proverbial duck to water, made 56. Brearley had gone LBW for just 2 and batting at 3, Radley was caught for 8, so Gooch and Gower batted together for the first time and put on 101 for the third wicket of an England total of 364. It was enough for England to win by an innings and 120 runs. Botham made 108 and took 8 wickets for just 34 in the Pakistan second innings.

As so often in his mercurial Test career Botham took the headlines but Gooch and Gower had done enough and had looked sufficiently the part to be retained for the third Test at Headingley.

The summer of 1978 was a miserable one for weather. Over 19 hours were lost in the Headingley Test and the match was drawn without even two innings' being completed. In England's only innings of 119 for 7, chasing a Pakistan total of 201, Gower with 39 and Gooch with 20 were the two top England scorers; both were out LBW to Sarfraz.

There was then a three Test series against New Zealand and both Gooch and Gower played in all three Tests. In the first, at the Oval, Gooch was dismissed third ball in the first innings for naught – he was LBW for the third successive time, but Gower, in only his fourth Test innings made his maiden Test hundred; he was run out for England's 'bogey' score - 111.

It is interesting to note that it was to take both the other two G's significantly longer before they were to pass the magic three figures. It took Gooch 36 innings and Gatting 54 innings, although Gooch got extremely close in the second innings of the first Test at the Oval when having made a duck in the first innings he finished on 91 not out in England's 7 wicket win.

Again Gooch and Gower batted together putting on 31 and getting England within sight of victory before Gower was caught for 11. Mike Brearley was not making runs and for the second Test Gooch was to be joined as opener by the second of his 16 opening partners, Geoffrey Boycott.

In their first opening partnership together they put on 111; Boycott made 131 on his return and Gooch made 55. Brearley dropped down the order to 5. Gower made 46 in an England total of 429 and England won by an innings. Botham took 9 wickets in the match.

So to Lord's for the third and final Test, England won by 7 wickets. Gooch made just 2 in England's first innings and Gower a somewhat streaky 71, second only to Radley's 77. In England's second innings Gooch and Gower again batted together and again got England to within sight of their victory target of 118 with a partnership of 70 runs for the third wicket before Gower was caught for 46. Gooch, however, was beginning to enjoy 'not outs' and finished with 42 not out.

In the intervening years since his difficult debut Gooch had continued to score heavily for Essex primarily as an opener scoring 1,273 runs at 42.43 in 1976, and 837 runs at 27.00 in 1977 and in 1978 for the second Test at Lord's against Pakistan and with England now under the captaincy of Mike Brearely he had returned as an England player – this time in his preferred position as opener.

David Gower had made his debut in the first Test at Edgbaston and therefore was joined by Gooch and so they played together for the first time and for the rest of the season.

In the years between Gooch's first Test and his recall, Kerry Packer had arrived on the cricketing scene. Recruiting some of the world's finest cricketers from all over the cricketing world to a 'world series' cricket competition outside the auspices of the governing bodies of the game and causing court battles broken friendships and a whole new evaluation of the financial worth of international cricket and cricketers.

Gooch, however, despite the loss of several class England players to the 'Packer circus' as it was to become known, was I believe selected on outright merit, as was Gower. He had recorded his highest score to date in his eighth Test innings and England had won. He had been retained for the third drawn Test against Pakistan at Leeds and for the whole of the three match series versus New Zealand.

England won all three Tests and Gooch was becoming established in the England side, as was Gower. Gooch having started with a naught in the first innings at the Oval, then made 91 not out, 55, 2 and 42 not out. Gooch finished the international summer of 1978 with 264 runs including three 50s and an average of 52.80. He had done enough to convince the selectors to include him for the winter tour to Australia.

With Gower scoring 153 runs in just three innings against Pakistan and 285 runs including his maiden Test hundred (111) against New Zealand in 5 innings at an average of 54.75 there was little doubt that he too would be on the plane to Australia.

They had both seemingly arrived and were established as England cricketers. England, with Botham rampant and under Brearley's brilliant captaincy, had beaten Pakistan 2 – 0 and beaten New Zealand 3 – 0.

Gatting, however, had failed to interest the selectors and had finished the 1978 domestic season with 1,166 runs at an average of 33.31 including 6, 50's and 2, 100's with a top score of 128 and had taken 19 catches for Middlesex.

So still Gooch, Gower and Gatting had not played in the same side for England. By the end of the 1978 season Gooch had played seven Tests, Gower had played six Tests and Gatting had played two Tests. Gooch and Gower had played five times in the same England team.

Gooch had scored 301 runs in 11 innings with a top score of 91 not out, average 33.44. Gower had scored 438 runs with a top score of 111 and an average of 54.75 and Gatting had scored just 11 runs in three innings.

1978/79
Versus Australia

If England were struggling in the Packer era so even more so were the Australians. Australia was the venue for the winter tour of 1978/79. With 'World series' cricket in full flood many people regarded this as a second class series with so many perceived 'first choice' Australian players not available. Tell that if you dare to England! With a fairly strong and settled side led by Mike Brearley, they won the series by five Tests to one.

Gooch opened in the first two Tests with Boycott but with scores of 2, 2, 1 and 43 dropped down to number four for the remaining four Tests of the series. Gower also played all six Tests; so two of the three G's had come together for England. Gooch had scored only 246 runs with a top score of 74 and Gower had scored 420 runs with a top score of 102. All three – Gooch, Gower and Gatting had by this time played for England, but never yet together.

England won the first Test at Brisbane by 7 wickets Gooch made just two in each innings again opening with Boycott but Gower having made 44 in the first innings this time saw England to victory recording his first not out – 48. Gooch bowled his first over in Test cricket in Australia's first innings for just one run.

At Perth, England again won comfortably by 166 runs. In England's first innings of 309, Gooch made just a single but Gower scored his second Test hundred (102). He was now therefore leading Gooch by two hundreds to nil. Gooch however was catching well; usually at slip he took 3 in this match. At this stage of their careers Gooch had taken 9 catches and Gower, more often in the covers had taken none.

England lost the third Test at Melbourne by 103 runs. Captain Brearley, having made just 36 runs in the previous two Tests, decided to return to opening and Gooch, having made just 44 runs moved down to number 4, with Gower batting at 5. In a low scoring match Brearley made 1 and naught; Gooch 25 and 40, in both cases being second highest England scorer behind Gower who made 29 and 49. Again they played well in partnership – 63 in the first innings and over 50 in the second innings.

For the fourth Test the batting order was retained and in a rare occasion neither player made significant contributions. Gooch made just 18 and 22; Gower 7 and 34. Derek Randall in England's second innings made a wonderful 150 and England won by 93 runs.

An unchanged side, with an unchanged batting order traveled to Adelaide for the fifth Test and having been put into bat by Australia found themselves at 27 for 5. Gooch caught off Hogg for 1 and Gower LBW for 9. England were dismissed for 169 but hit back by dismissing the Australians for 164 Botham taking 4-42 having top-scored for England with 74. England made a decent second innings score – 360 – and won the Test by 205 runs again bowling Australia out cheaply. In England's second innings Gooch made 18 and Gower 21.

So to Sydney for the sixth and final Test.

Again Gooch batted at 4 and Gower at 5. Having bowled Australia out very cheaply for just 198 runs – Botham 4-57 this time the two G's both performed well. Yet again they were the leading scorers in England's first innings total of 308. Gooch scored 74 before being stumped – one of only two occasions when he was dismissed in this manner and Gower 65. These were the two highest scores for England in the match. They put on nearly 80 runs for England's fourth wicket. England won the Test by 9 wickets.

At the end of the tour Gooch had scored 246 runs at an average of 22.36 and Gower topped England's batting with 420 runs at 42.00. Both players returned home with reputations enhanced and futures bright.

1979
Versus India

In the summer of 1979 England were to play a four Test series against India after the Prudential one-day World cup which was won comfortably by the West Indies beating England at Lord's.

The Indian side was captained by Venkat and included the likes of Gavaskar, Viswanath, Kapil Dev and Chandrasekhar.

For the first Test at Edgbaston, England, captained by Brearley, continued with their policy of Gooch and Gower at 4 and 5 respectively. England scored 633 for 5 declared in their only innings and won the Test by an innings and 83 runs, Gooch scored 83 and Gower made exactly 200 not out It was to be his second highest score in Test match cricket They put on a partnership of nearly 200 runs.. England put on 145 for the third wicket and over 190 for the fourth. Botham took 7 wickets in the match, Mike Hendrick took 6 for 81 and Gooch bowled 6 overs for only 8 runs in India's second innings and held 4 catches in the match, the remaining three Tests where drawn.

Gooch and Gower played all four Tests. Gooch, a natural opener batted at number four or three throughout the series. Gower was still to take a catch for England. The second Test was played at Lord's and sadly over 8 hours of play were lost to bad weather and England having blown India away for just 96 in their first innings – Botham 5-35 - made over four hundred in their only innings.

Gower, perhaps in his pomp as an England batsman, top scored in the England innings with 82 and Gooch was bowled by Kapil Dev for just 10.

Both the G's however got 'firsts' – Gooch bowled 10 overs in India's first innings and took his first Test wicket and not a bad first, he had Gavaskar caught by Taylor for 42 the top score for India and Gower broke his catching duck when he caught Viswanath off Lever for 113 in India's second innings. Lord's is so often a graveyard for England's cricketing hopes but this match was at least an honourable draw. England had again decided to tinker with the batting order for this Test with Gooch moving to 3 and Gower to 4, and with Randall batting at 5.

It seemed, at least to me, that at this time England were in a dilemma as to whether they should play either Randall or Gatting and that there was not room for both in the England batting order.

The third Test at Headingley was again devastated by rain and in England's only innings of 270, Gooch, again batting at 3 was caught for 4 and Gower, batting at 4 made his first duck for England, LBW to Kapil Dev. Nearly three days play were lost to the wet conditions, England winning the toss and batting first made 270. Again Gooch 'turned his arm over, he bowled 3 overs for 2 runs and took a catch.

For the fourth and final Test at the Oval which was also drawn, England made changes. Randall was dropped, Brearley dropped himself down the batting order to 7, Peter Willey was recalled for his third Test and debut caps were awarded to the Yorkshire wicket-keeper batsman David Bairstow and the Surrey left handed opener Alan Butcher. In England's first innings of 305, Gooch top-scored with 79 but Gower made 0 in the first innings again LBW to Kapil Dev and just 7 in the second innings. Gooch, however, had a good Test, he made England's top score of 79 in England's first innings total of 305 and a useful 31 in the second when England were looking for quick runs. Bairstow made his Test best of 59.

This was the Test that saw perhaps one of the finest Test innings of all time. India set a daunting 438 to win, got to within 9 runs of victory with Gavaskar scoring 221 off 443 balls including 21 fours; a quite outstanding innings. Botham took 3-97 and Peter Willey bowled in excess of 40 overs. Gooch and Gower had retained their places at 3 and 4 in the order.

At the end of the series Gooch had made over 200 runs in 5 innings at 41.40 and Gower mainly due to his undefeated 200 scored 289 at 72.25 in five innings. Gower took one catch and Gooch 6.

    Still no place then for Gatting.

I have never quite understood the thinking behind the practice of picking a player for just the last Test of a series but it seemed to be almost an obligatory thing to do at this time. Alan Butcher was selected for his debut, opening with Boycott he made 14 and 20 and this was to be Butcher's only Test. Surely he deserved better.

1979/80
Versus Australia

With 'official' cricket still battling the so-called Packer revolution, England toured Australia for a three Test series. The West Indies toured at the same time and also played a three Test series as 'establishment cricket' attempted to fight back against Packer; sensibly England did not play for the famous Ashes urn as Australia were to win all three Tests: the first at Perth by 138 runs, the second at Sydney by 6 wickets and the third at Melbourne by 8 wickets.

Gooch and Gower both toured, Gower played all three Tests and Gooch played the last two, opening with Boycott. In the first Test it was the first time that Gower played without Gooch in the side; England went for Randall to open with Boycott the experiment did not work in that both openers made naught in the first innings but Boycott 'carried his bat' in England's second innings for – of all scores – 99 not out, England's number 11 was Willis who was caught for 0 and I wonder if those two have ever spoken since! England captain Brearley batted at 6, Australia won by 138 runs, Gower batting at four scored 17 and 23.

Australia then won the second Test by six wickets; Gooch was recalled to open with Boycott. In his 18 Tests to date this was the seventh time that Gooch had opened. England were again comfortably beaten and Gooch contributed just 18 and 4 runs. Gower batted at six in the first innings and made just 3, being one of Greg Chappell's 47 wickets in Tests. Brearley again used Gooch's medium pace swing bowling for 19 overs in the match. In Australia's first innings he took 2 wickets for 16 runs in 11 overs.

In the second innings batting at 7 because Derek Underwood had been promoted to do his famous night-watchman duties, Gower made 98 not out. Unfortunately history repeated itself in that Gower's last partner was Bob Willis, he was again dismissed by Lillee this time for 1 run having hung in with Gower whilst they put on 19 runs. Gower's 98 not out was the top score for England in the match, it was only equaled by Greg Chappell for Australia also with 98 not out. The next best England score was the brave 43 by night-watchman Derek Underwood.

England with Brearley at the helm, Boycott, Botham, Willis, Underwood and Taylor in the side as well as Gooch and Gower frankly should have been doing better and for the third Test Wayne Larkins of Norhants made his debut batting at three.

In the third Test at Melbourne, which Australia won by eight wickets, Gooch retained his place as opener and managed to run himself out for 99 in an England first innings total of 306. He had pushed a ball to mid-on and in desperation to reach his first Test hundred and with his wife looking on in the crowd set off for a crazy run. He failed to make his ground by a yard or so. Having therefore made his highest Test score to date, he then made, to his great credit, the second top-score of 51 in England's second innings, behind only to a wonderful unbeaten century (119) by Botham. Gower, batting at four, made 0 and 11. Only the third 'duck' in his Test career to date. It was his 29th innings for his country. But with Australia scoring 477 in their first innings and Lillee returning match figures of 11 for 138 England's fate was sealed.

For Gooch the disappointment must have been enormous. For England the disappointment was serious.

1979/80
Jubilee Test V. India

On the way home from Australia, England stopped off for a one-off Test celebrating the Golden Jubilee of the formation of the Board of Control for cricket in India. As so often with these types of games the match was disappointing.

Both Gooch and Gower played in this Jubilee Test against India in February 1980. In a Test dominated by Ian Botham - 114 runs and 13 wickets and Bob Taylor - with a record equaling 10 dismissals in the Test and scoring 43 runs in putting on 171 runs with Botham. England won by 10 wickets. Gooch opened and scored 8 and 49 not out and Gower batting at four in his only innings scored 16.

As was the way with Gooch at this stage of his career he was again used as an occasional bowler by Brearley bowling four overs in India's first innings for just 3 runs, he picked up his twenty second catch in India's second innings when he caught the Indian wicket-keeper Kirmani for a duck off the bowling of Botham – who else?

Mike Brearley stepped down as England captain expressing a desire to pursue a career outside cricket. It was not however to be the last time Brearley was to assume the mantle of England captain. He is probably one of the very best Captains England has ever had.

1980
Versus West Indies

In the summer of 1980 England under the new captain Ian Botham were to face the might of the West Indies. The West Indies had no Walcott, Worrell or Weekes but they did have an awesome bowling attack of Marshall, Holding, Roberts and Garner and an equally awesome batting attack including Greenidge, Haynes, Richards and Kallicharan, captained by Clive Lloyd.

England lost the first Test by 2 wickets and the remaining four were all drawn. Graham Gooch opened in all five Tests with Boycott and David Gower was to play only the first Test due to injury. He was in effect replaced by Mike Gatting. Still the three G's had not made it onto the field together for England.

Gatting had scored heavily for Middlesex and was undoubtedly worthy of his recall. In the second Test at Lord's and in his thirty sixth innings for England Gooch got his first hundred for England also becoming the first batsman that season to pass 1,000 runs. He made 123 in England's first innings and 47 in the second. Again the great English weather played its part in the Test with nearly ten hours being lost. Gatting in his first Test innings since the 77-78 tour in New Zealand scored 18 batting at 5.

For the third Test in Manchester, England made changes Larkins and Rose replacing Tavare and Woolmer in the batting but Gatting stayed at 5 and with the third day being washed out England again got a draw. Gooch scored just 28 runs in the match but Gatting having scored 33 in England's first innings total of a mere 150, second only to 70 by Rose, passed 50 for the first time in England's second innings in making 56.

Incredibly the third day of the fourth Test at the Oval was again a wash out. Gooch made 83 in England's first innings of 370 but 0 in the second. Gatting got to 48 in England's first innings and made 15 in the second.

For the fifth Test again the weather in what was to be a rotten summer for rain even by England standards played the major role. There was no play possible on either the first or fourth days play. Gooch made 55 in England's second innings but Gatting made just 1 run in each innings. Gooch again bowled in the West Indies only innings and again proved more than useful in picking up 2 wickets for just 18 runs in 8 overs.

Centenary Test
Versus Australia
The first time

This season of climactic discontent ended with a celebratory Test against Australia to mark a hundred years of Tests between the two nations in England.

For the first time the three G's were to play in the same Test side. The weather and some rather pernickety and fussy umpiring ruined the match. Over 10 hours were again lost to weather but this was after all a one-off celebratory Test with little else at stake. Surely both players and umpires could and should have tried harder to play more cricket.

Lord's, August, against the oldest of Test enemies was perhaps fitting that here came for the first time together in Test match cricket the three G's.

Gooch, by now becoming established as an opener having batted in several positions for England, had already played twenty five Tests and scored over 1,000 runs; he opened with Boycott. Gower who had played twenty one Tests and had also scored well over a 1,000 runs came back into the side at 4 and Gatting who had played just six Tests and scored just 183 runs kept his place at 5. Whilst it was to be the first time Gooch, Gower and Gatting were to play together for England, the Test is also notable for the last ever broadcast by John Arlott after 35 years as a Test match commentator. When the ground tanoy on the final afternoon of the Test announced that Arlott had completed his last radio Test match commentary, even Boycott on his way to an undefeated 128 and passing 7,000 runs in Tests laid down his bat to join the entire ground and all the players in applauding him.

Of the three G's, Gooch made just 8 and 15, falling to Lillee on both occasions; Gower made 45 and 35 and Gatting having made just 12 in the first innings was 51 not out in the second. So the three G's played together for the first time. In a rain-ruined match they scored a combined total of 167 runs for 5 times out. Gatting took a catch and Gooch bowled eight wicket-less overs. The match ended in a disappointing draw.

By the end of the summer of 1980 Gooch in twenty six Test innings had scored 1,346 runs and was averaging 33.65 with a top score of 123, Gower had scored 1,416 runs in 34 innings with a top score of 200 not out and an average of 44.25 and Gatting in seven Tests and after just 12 innings with a top score of 56 was averaging 22.36.

Gooch with his more than useful right arm swing bowling had taken 6 wickets at 36.17. So what of their first class career averages at the end of 1980? Gatting in 25 innings had scored 880 runs at 41.90 with 2 hundreds and 4 fifties, Gooch 1,437 runs at 47.90 with 6 hundreds and 2 fifties in 35 innings and Gower 1,142 runs at 32.62 with 2 100's and 3 fifties in 36 innings.

1980/81
Versus West Indies
Oh what a 'lovely' tour!

All 3, Gooch, Gower and Gatting were selected for the winter tour to the West Indies. Sport and politics do not mix. In 1980/81 England toured the West Indies and a difficult and troubled tour is probably as best remembered for events off the field as on it. This was a terrible time for England, English cricket and the world of international Test cricket. South Africa was in the sporting wilderness, banned from all international sport because of apartheid.

It was an irony that the tour should be to the West Indies; a group of separate but fiercely proud countries that came together as one cricketing nation; each with a sad history as victims of the abomination that had been the slave trade.

An injury to Bob Willis, England's vice-captain and iconic fast bowler on whom so much rested, saw the Surrey bowler Robin Jackman, who had played and coached in South Africa, who had a home in South Africa and was married to a South African called into the squad. The result was that the second Test scheduled to be played in Guyana did not happen as the Gyananese authorities revoked Jackman's permit.

After much political discussions regarding the 'Gleneagles Agreement' and many faxes and telephone calls; the tour did continue. The West Indian side of the time was possibly at its most powerful with Greenidge, Haynes, Richards and Lloyd in a power-house batting line up and Roberts and Holding leading a fearful pace attack backed by the likes of Croft, Joel Garner and Marshall.

In the first Test in Trinidad, England captained by Ian Botham had been steam-rollered to an innings defeat, bowled out for just 178 and 169 in reply to the West Indies first innings total of 426. Gooch scored 41 and 5, Gower 48 and 27 and the doggedly determined Boycott had made 30 and 70.

As if all the previous off-field shenanigans were not enough the death on the second evening of the Test of England's assistant manager, coach and 'father' of the side – Ken Barrington of a heart attack was probably the worst thing that had ever happened to most of these young and dedicated England cricketers.

For this third and tragic Test at Barbados, of all places the home of the three W's, Gatting came into the side replacing Rose to join Gooch and Gower for only the second time the three G's played together. I suspect that none of the three wanted to be there. It was in this Test that Graham Gooch perhaps produced one of the most character-full and gutsy performances of his Test career scoring a hundred in England's second innings.

In England's first innings of a paltry 122 all out he had been equal top scorer with 26. Needing 522 in their second innings to win the Test, Gooch scored 116 Gower scored a fifty and was England's second top scorer. Gatting, batting at three made just 2 and naught. The Test perhaps not surprisingly was badly lost by England and the three G's were again split up with the dropping of Gatting, he was not to play again in the remaining two Tests on the tour. Both of which were drawn, and many speculated that his brief stop-start Test career was over.

Gooch in particular battled on bravely for the remainder of the tour. In the fourth Test in Antigua he scored 116 runs in the match and Gower scored over 50. In the final Test in Jamaica Gooch scored 153 in England's first innings total of 285 all out. In England's second innings Gower made an equally forceful 154 not out in an England total of 302 for 6 declared. It was to be Gower's highest score against the West Indies.

Gooch returned to England having topped the Test averages in scoring 460 runs at 57.50, with Gower second with 376 runs at 53.71. England had lost the series 2-0 and the three G's had only played twice together - without a win.

1981 and 1981/82
Versus Australia and India

The home summer of 1981 saw an 'Ashes' tour by Australia and it is to Gatting's credit that he was to regain his Test place. By the end of 1981 he finished eighth in the first class averages with 1,492 runs at an average of 55.28 with 4 hundreds.

For the first Test at Nottingham the three came together for England again. This time they were to play together for the first five of the six Test series. Gatting averaged over 30 in six Tests, Gower only 25 in 5 and Gooch perhaps as a result of the difficulties of the winter less than 14. So it was ironic that the least well-established of the three G's was the most successful and they had played now for five Tests in a row.

This was of course the summer of Ian Botham and the extraordinary events at Headingley when England following-on came back to win the Test that put Cricket on front, back and middle pages. After defeat by 4 wickets at Nottingham, when Gatting was England's top scorer with 52 in England's first innings and Gower made 54 runs in the match and then a draw at Lord's when Botham made a pair, Botham either resigned or was stripped of the captaincy – it depends on whose account you read! Mike Brearley was recalled as captain.

In the match Gooch scored 44 and 20, Gower made 27 and his eight Test match fifty (89), and Gatting 59 – his fourth Test fifty and his highest score for England to date and 16. The third Test has gone down in the history of sport, not just cricket, when having been forced to follow on they won by just 18 runs. Gooch scored just 2 runs in the match, Gower 33 and Gatting 16 runs.

The fourth Test was won by England, Gooch dropped back to number four. England won a Test without one player on either side passing 50. Gooch scored 21 runs in each innings.

The fifth Test was won by England, none of the three G's made a contribution, although Gatting for only the second time bowled in Tests – 3 overs for 13 runs. The sixth Test was drawn and neither Gooch nor Gower played. Gatting however scored over 50 runs in both innings for the first time in his Test career.

England however had won the series and all three G's were on the plane for England's winter tour to India. Again they were to play five of the six Tests together.

1981/82
Versus India

If the previous tour to West Indies had been bad for the problems off the field this tour was to plummet the depths of Test cricket for activity - if that is the right word – on the field. India won the first Test and the rest of the tour descended into quite literally a slow grinding dirge of unacceptable over-rates on unacceptably dead and boring wickets backed by ordinary umpiring and could have sounded the death-knell of Test cricket on the most fanatical cricketing continent on the planet.

Brearley had re-retired and the side was now captained by Keith Fletcher. Fletcher had returned to England colours after having missed 47 England Tests.

India's bowling strength remained with their spinners, although Kapil Dev had now emerged as a genuine pace bowler and all-rounder. England, captained by Keith Fletcher who was to get into trouble for clipping his stumps when having been given out to a dubious decision, one of many to go against England on the tour possibly set the tone for the whole of the tour with a definite 'siege mentality' that pervaded the whole tour party. England took a battery of quick and medium pace bowlers including Willis, Dilley, Allott, Botham and Lever! Emburey and Underwood were the core of England's spin attack and they played together in three of the six Tests.

The first Test at Bombay was won by India by 138 runs. England were bowled out for just 102 in their second innings, their lowest ever score to date in India. No player on either side made 100, Boycott top-scored the match with 60 in England's first innings total of just 166. Gooch scored 3 runs in the match, and Gower 25. On the first day of the third Test at Delhi India bowled just

78 overs and in Madras slow bowlers Doshi and Shastri managed all of 9 overs in an hour!

All three G's bowled during the series and Gower picked up his only Test wicket in the sixth test at Kanpur when in a rain affected match he had Kapil Dev caught by Dilley for 116. In the previous Test in India's second innings England used ten bowlers, including the wicketkeeper Taylor when Gooch took the gloves. They would probably have used all eleven if Allott had not been off the field injured. Each of Gooch, Gower and Gatting bowled in the same Test for the only time. This tells perhaps the whole tale of a sad and disappointing tour. However it was as batsmen that the three G's had been selected and again their fortunes were mixed. Gooch top scored with 487 runs at 54.11, Gower scored 375 at 46.87 but Gatting struggled making only 68 runs in 6 innings at an average of just 13.60.

Gooch opened throughout the series, with Boycott in the first four Tests and with Tavare in the fifth Test at Madras. Boycott played the last of his 108 Tests at Calcutta. He set records for the most number of runs 8,114 and Test innings (193), perhaps inadvertently setting a challenge for Gooch himself.

Gower batted at 4 but Gatting, who missed the first Test but played in all the remaining five Tests ensuring that the three G's again played five Tests together, in six innings batted at 8, 7,8,7,6 and 6. In the second Test Gooch scored 58 and 40, Gower 82 and 32 not out and Gatting made 29 in his only innings. In the third Test Gooch scored 91 runs for once out and Gower having seen Tavare make 149 and Boycott pass 8000, a world test record for the time runs in scoring 105, made 0.

It could be argued that Gooch and Gower were becoming established in England colours but that Gatting was still to make his mark and to convince the selectors of his International credentials. He had scored 797 runs in twenty two Tests with a top score of 59.

England ended the tour with the first ever Test for Sri Lanka in Colombo. Gooch and Gower played, Gatting did not. England recorded a comfortable win by 7 wickets Gower made 131 runs for only once out.

1982
South African Breweries Strike

Sport and money have to mix and with South Africa in the sporting wilderness, South African Breweries had dug deep into their pockets to procure Packer like unsanctioned tours by international cricketers. In March 1982 an 'England' team toured South Africa paid for and sponsored by South African Breweries and this team included Graham Gooch along with other England players – Larkins, who had been ignored for the previous winter's tour, Boycott, Knott, Emburey and Underwood. Many of the players who went on this tour either believed that their England careers were coming to an end or that they were unlikely to become England regulars. Why Gooch, probably the most established player with a long-term England future, decided to join this 'rebel' tour only he can answer but the result was that he, along with all the other 'tourists' received a three year ban from Test cricket and therefore did not play for England for thirty one Tests; it should be noted that as soon as Gooch became available to England he was immediately recalled. So for the next thirty one Tests and three years the three G's could not play in the same England side. Gower however was an ever-present in the side but Gatting still was to become a regular. While Gooch was in exile Gower played in all of England's Tests and Gatting just sixteen. It was also during this period that David Gower became England captain. The first of the three G's to achieve this. In 1982 at Lord's he had taken the role versus Pakistan when Willis withdrew with a neck injury. England had lost. He also passed 3,000 Test runs on the tour to Australia in 1982-83.
He again took the captaincy against Pakistan at Faislabad on the 1983/84 tour, when again Willis was unwell. The Test was drawn and Gower made 152 in England's only innings, taking him past 4,000 Test runs. He retained the captaincy for the final Test in Lahore. The match was drawn. Gower made 173 not out

in the second innings. Gatting had played in all three of the Gower captaincy Tests to date.

1982
Versus India and Pakistan.

Keith Fletcher's brief reign as England captain had ended and the Mantle now passed back to England stalwart Bob Willis.
England won the India series one Test to nil with the other two drawn. Only Gower of the three G's played. Gatting however rejoined Gower for the three Tests against Pakistan. England won the series two Tests to one. In six Tests Gower had scored 304 runs in 11 innings and Gatting 111 runs in 6 innings.

1982/83
Versus Australia

Only Gower of the three G's toured Australia this Winter. Gooch was still banned of course. Australia won two Tests to one. Gatting was not selected, England took Lamb, Tavare, and Randall as the core of their middle-order and top order batting. It seemed to me, that at the time Derek Randall and Mike Gatting were an either or selection. Rarely did the two play together.

1983
Versus New Zealand

England played a four match series against New Zealand after the third Prudential World Cup. England still captained by Willis won the series three Tests to one. Gower, now an ever present, played all four Tests and Gatting again came in from the cold and played the last two Tests. David Gower scored consecutive hundreds. In the second innings of the second Test he made 112 out of an England total of 252 – the next highest England score was 28 by Lamb, and he then made 108 in the first innings of the third Test.; the next best score being 51. In the summer of 1983

Gower had scored over 400 runs in 8 innings and Gatting 121 runs in 4 innings, including his highest test score to date of 81.

1983/84
Versus New Zealand & Pakistan

England toured New Zealand for three Tests and Pakistan for three Tests in this winter and both Gower and Gatting were in the squad. They played together in the first two Tests against New Zealand, and in all three Tests against Pakistan. Gower captained England for the last two Tests against Pakistan and Gatting was used as an opener for the Pakistan series.

England lost in New Zealand, it was their first series defeat against New Zealand. The rubber against Pakistan was also lost by one Test to nil. In a disappointing winter for England, Gower had scored 449 runs in Pakistan in 5 innings, of which 334 were made as captain and only 79 in New Zealand. Gatting had scored just 38 runs in New Zealand and 158 in Pakistan.

1984
Versus West Indies
The Captain's Curse

In 1984 the then all-powerful West Indies toured England. Gower was formally appointed as captain of England. The West Indies squad included Richards, Greenidge, Haynes, Lloyd, Marshall, Holding and Garner!

England where humiliated losing all five Tests. England used over twenty players in the series. Gatting played only the one Test – the second at his home ground Lord's, making 1 and 29. The season ended with the first Test in England against Sri Lanka. A disinterested and disillusioned England were held to a draw.

In 1984/85 England toured India. Gower was still captain, Gooch was still banned and Gatting, regarded as one of the best of players' of spin bowling in the country was selected.

Having lost the first Test in Bombay England made an impressive come back winning in Delhi and Madras and Gatting finally arrived as a truly credible Test batsman. In the second innings of the first Test, and after 54 innings Gatting scored his first England hundred – 136. In the fourth Test at Madras, batting at 3 he scored 207. In a record England score at the time against India of 652 for 7 declared Graham Fowler joined in the fun in making 201, the first time two England batsmen had made double hundreds in the same innings they put on a record partnership of 241 for the second wicket.

Gower whilst having a less than good time with the bat had won his first Tests and his first series as captain. They both played all five Tests. Gower was England captain, Gooch was due to return from his South African ban and Gatting had scored 575 runs at an average of 95.83.

1985 v. Australia
'The Return of the Three'

In 1985 England played Australia. Gooch was out of exile and available and was immediately recalled. Gower established as captain and Gatting who had played in the previous five Tests of England's tour to India and had had a tremendous tour retained his place. Gatting returned from India surely now an established Test player whose credentials where no longer in doubt. He had topped the batting averages scoring 527 runs at an astonishing average of 95.83 with a top score of 207, it was perhaps typical of the determined character of the man that it had taken him 54 innings to score his maiden century for England but that he should then make a double hundred on the same tour.

Captain Gower finished the tour with only one fifty and a disappointing average of 27.83 but crucially had led England to a 2-1 series victory having lost the first Test.

England had also won the by now standard one-day series by four games to one. The international one-day game was becoming increasingly dominant in cricket and players such as the three G's had to be able to perform consistently in both forms. Whether the three W's would have been able to be as dominant in one day cricket as they were in Test cricket we will never know; but this was an extra pressure on the three G's.

International cricket at this time was reaching a point of being almost 'non stop', with one day and Test matches piling in on each other and the pressure to perform piling on the players.

I still however feel that Weekes, Worrell and Walcott would have thrived in the one-day format of the game.

During the period of the Gooch exile Gower had played all thirty two Tests, he had scored 2,105 runs in 56 innings with 5 not outs at an average of 41.27 including fourteen Tests as captain. Gatting had played exactly half the Tests during the absence of Gooch, in 16 matches he had scored 1,033 runs in 29 innings with 5 not outs at an average of 43.04.

So the three G's came together in the same Test side for only the tenth time, against the oldest of adversaries – Australia.

The first Test was played at Headingley and England won by 5 wickets. Of the three only Gatting with 53 runs in England's first innings made any significant contribution; Gooch however picked up 2 of his total of 23 Test wickets – Hilditch was caught, Downton for 119 and Boon LBW for 14, giving Gooch figures of 2 for 57 off 21 overs.

At Lord's in the second Test all three were retained and the match was lost by four wickets. England lose at Lord's – no surprise there then! In the match Gooch, opening, made 47 runs, Gower, batting at three scored over a hundred runs in the match and Gatting – batting at 4 in the first innings and 6 in the second made nearly 90 runs for once out.

For the first time all three were to play a full series together.

The third and fourth Tests were drawn. In the third Test at Trent Bridge Gooch made 70 and 48. Captain Gower batting at three produced one of his finest innings of 166 in England's first innings and Gatting also scored well; he was run out for 74 in the first innings and was not out 35 in the second.

England scored 652 runs for 12 wickets in the match and the three G's contributed 410 of them.

In the fourth (drawn) Test at Old Trafford the three again scored runs; in England's only innings of 482 for 9 declared Gooch made 74, Gower 47 in passing 5,000 runs for his country and Gatting – surely by now reveling in his role as an established England player made what was to be his best score against Australia – 160, it was his first century for England in England after 40 innings, he also bowled 4 overs in Australia's second innings (none for 14).

England then won the fifth Test at Edgbaston by an innings. Gower scored 215, it was to be his best ever Test score, and Gatting made his second consecutive century, exactly 100 not out – allowing Gower to declare on 595 for five. The Kent medium pace swing bowler Richard Ellison sealed the match for England with 10 wickets for 104 in the match.

In the sixth Test, won by England by an innings and 94 runs Gooch 196 and Gower 157 recorded a partnership of 351 runs, in an England first innings total of 464, by far and away the best any of the three G's were to produce in partnership. The next highest score in the innings was 50 in extras!

Gatting, however, despite failing in this match was perhaps at his best. Confidence boosted by the confidence shown in him by the selectors and his team-mates. He scored over a hundred runs in the third Test, scored 160 in the first innings of the fourth Test at Manchester and another – unbeaten hundred in the fifth Test at Birmingham.

At the end of the series Gatting again topped the averages – 527 runs at 87.83, Gower was second 732 at 81.33 and Gooch too had averaged over 50. In 27 innings the three G's had scored 1,746 out of an England total of 3,132 runs in the series, they had effectively dominated the England batting in 1985. Now they could challenge the three W's – or could they?

So, at the end of the 1985 series against Australia the three G's, having played the entire series together, had played a total of eighteen Tests together. Gooch had scored 1,276 runs at an average of 42.53 with 3 100's and 6 50's, Gower had scored 1,483 runs at 51.12 with 3 100's and 7 50's and Gatting had scored 921 runs at 40.04 with 2 100's and 7 50's. Combined, the three G's had therefore scored 3,680 runs with 8 100s and 20 50s, between them the three G's had held 27 catches and Gooch had taken 4 wickets.

The records of the three W's after the same number of Tests together (18) were as follows: Walcott 29 completed innings scoring 1,111 runs with 4 hundreds, 3 50s at an average of 42.73, Weekes had scored 1,666 runs at 57.45 in 29 completed innings, with 5 hundreds and 16 50's. Worrell was averaging 58.25 having scored 1,631 runs in 28 innings with 5 hundreds and 6 fifties, he had also taken 26 wickets at 36.85. Add to that the fact that Walcott had already taken 2 wickets, and had taken 23 catches – mainly as a wicket-keeper the W's had taken 28 wickets.

Worrell had held 17 catches and Weekes 19.

Between them the three W's had scored 4,408 runs including no less than 14 hundreds and 25 fifties. They had held 59 catches – 20 of them by Walcott as wicket-keeper.

The three W's were surely well ahead on points.

1985/86
Versus the West Indies.
Oh No Not Again!

So to the England winter tour to the West Indies, the home of the three W's. If the previous tour to the West Indies had been difficult and tragic with the 'Jackman affair' and the death of Ken Barrington; this tour in cricketing terms and with politics still prevalent was an unmitigated disaster.

The West Indies recorded an unprecedented 5-0 series victory at home, following their 5-0 demolition of England in England. They simply overwhelmed England with batting power – Vivian Richards scoring the fastest ever Test hundred to date in the fifth Test in Antigua, supported by Greenidge, Haynes, Richardson and Gomes plus the pace bowling of Marshall and Garner who set records by taking 27 wickets apiece supported by Walsh, Patterson and Holding. Ian Botham, captained by Gower, was becoming almost as famous for his supposed antics off the field as his performances on it.

The press went to the tour in force; and sadly they were not all cricket journalists. It seems that at times an undeclared state of open warfare existed between the players and the press.

Gooch was under extraordinary pressure due to his earlier South African Breweries tour and even threatened to leave the tour at one stage. He had captained the tour to South Africa but there where other players who had accompanied him to South Africa who where also on this tour: Emburey, Willey and Taylor.

With horrible echoes of the previous tour, much was said and made of his South African adventure by some, mainly obscure West Indian politicians and some demonstrators. Gooch it must be said was the ultimate unhappy tourist. He took the criticisms to heart, and perhaps feeling unsupported by the rest of the team and management I wonder if this was the start of a rift between Gooch and Gower.

They where perceived to have so different attitudes to the way to captain, manage and play international cricket. Gower also took fearful stick in the press for his perceived 'laid back' attitude and 'voluntary nets' theories.

Botham and Lamb were basically and sometimes literally sticking two fingers up to all and sundry. As for Gatting; his tour started and virtually ended, when in the pre Test one-day match in Jamaica he had his nose rearranged by a fearsome delivery from Marshall, the injury was so bad it required him to fly home for surgery. It was a very nasty injury and it has been reported that after Gatting left the field the bowler handed the ball to the umpire saying that he could not possibly bowl with it as it had not only got Gatting's blood still on it but also a piece of his nose-bone imbedded in it.

With Gower's captaincy under scrutiny – totally unfairly in my opinion, with Gooch under huge pressure and ready to leave the tour at any moment, with every move of Ian Botham being scrutinised in a totally unfair way, with a rampant press, competing viciously against each other and therefore never letting the truth get in the way of a good if unfounded story, an injury of such seriousness to Gatting got an horrendous tour off to a great start!

It is a measure of the man that he returned to rejoin the tour party; a tour party bludgeoned, shattered, disheartened and totally beaten. Most men would and could have stayed well away from such mayhem without a murmur of comment even from the then rampant British press; but not Gatting he was selected for the final Test in Antigua, the scene of Viv Richards astonishing 56 ball hundred. He faced a bowling attack of: Marshall, Patterson, Garner and Holding! He scored 15 and 1, but frankly his mere presence was far more important and significant than his scores.

Any lingering trust and honesty between the press and the players almost completely broken down with papers sending people simply to follow the off-field activities or lack of them rather than report on England's dire on-field performances. England took the best squad available but the batsmen could not consistently stand up to the battery of fast bowling, and, with the bowling totally lacking the equivalent pace or penetration there was only ever to be one winner.

This was a miserable tour for England and the three G's were on it and indeed in it! To their credit Gower was first in the averages with 370 runs at 37.00 and Gooch second with 276 runs at 27.60

The first Test in Jamaica saw the West Indies complete a ten wicket victory. England were bowled out for just 159 and 152 having chosen to bat. Gooch made 51 in the first innings and the writing was probably on the wall when you look at the match figures of the West Indian bowlers: Marshall 5-59, Garner 5-80, Patterson 7-74 and Holding a mere 3-88.

The second Test was business as usual for the West Indies: England beaten by 7 wickets. The top score for England in the match was made by Gower who made 66. The third Test in Barbados was lost by England by an innings. England scored just 189 and 199.

Gooch and Gower, however, were standing firm. Gooch made another brave 50 and Gower again top scored with – again – 66. The fourth Test was won by the West Indies by 10 wickets.

Marshall 5 wickets, Garner 7 wickets, Patterson 3 wickets and Holding 5 wickets. Gatting showing the grit and courage that was to be his hallmark returned from his badly broken nose to play in the last Test at Antigua.

The West Indies won by 240 runs. Gooch made 51 in each innings and Gower the top score by an English batsman in the entire series – 90 runs in England's total of 310.

So, due to fate and serious injury the three G's only played the one Test together. So the three G's coming to perhaps the best of their careers were still, by injury, politics and selectorial whim not to be playing regularly together.

1986
Versus India and New Zealand.

Having faced the power and might of the West Indies England returned for the summer of 1986 to face two three Test series against firstly India and then New Zealand. However, shell-shocked and disillusioned as they may have been after the winter in the West Indies they may have looked forward to a more relaxing series of the English summer; however it all went sadly wrong. England failed to win a single Test and managed to lose twice to India and once to New Zealand.

The three G's played together in five of the six Tests and, in an extraordinarily badly handled situation, Peter May, chairman of England's selectors, and appearing to act with less subtlety than a rattlesnake passed the captaincy (after the first Test at Lord's had been lost by England by 5 wickets) from one 'G' - Gower to another - Gatting. All three G's played in this first Test which India won by 5 wickets. Gooch perhaps with a point to prove top scored in the match for England with 114 in their first innings when Gatting made a duck. So Mike Gatting, after 43 Tests and having been in and out of the England side and having batted all over the place when trying to become established as an England Test player, was now passed the 'poisoned chalice' of captain of his country. In a demoralised, disillusioned and disappointing

England side under the charge of, in my opinion, a very poor and inconsistent group of selectors, Gatting became the second of the three G's to captain England.

He began his reign as England captain - without the deposed Gower - in the second Test at Headingley and presided over England's seventh successive defeat, which saw one of the largest winning margins for an Indian victory over England.

England made paltry scores of just 102 and 128. One Roger Binny took 7 wickets in the match. Gooch scored just 13 runs and Gatting was second top scorer in the first innings with all of 13 runs and then found himself top scorer with 31 not out, batting at 5 he watched as his England team surrendered 6 wickets for 38 runs.

The third Test saw, rightly, the return of Gower. The match was drawn. Gatting made 183 in England's first innings (his fifth hundred) – it was to be his highest Test score in England. The next best score in the match was 79 by India's Amarnath. In a rare event both India and England scored exactly the same total – 390 – in their first innings. In India's second innings Gatting brought himself on to bowl – 2 overs for 10 runs. Gooch scored 0 and 40 and Gower 49 and 26. So Gatting responded to captaincy by topping the averages against India with 73.25. Gooch was second averaging only 29.16 and Gower third at just 25.25.

All three G's played the three Test series against New Zealand, which England lost by one Test to nil. The first Test at Lord's was drawn, in the second innings Gooch matched Gatting with 183, Gower made 62 in the first innings. Gatting failed – scoring just 2 and 26. Perhaps as a sign of his down to earth character Gatting may have showed his down to earth sense of humour in that he bowled Gower in the second innings (1 over for 1 run) and used Gooch, more pragmatically, in the first innings He bowled 13 overs, 6 maidens and took the wicket of Bruce Edgar, conceding just 23 runs. England lost by eight wickets at Trent Bridge. Sir Richard Hadlee took ten wickets in the match. Only Gower of the three, with 97 runs in the match, performed. The third Test at the Oval was effectively ruined by rain and was drawn giving New Zealand their first series win in England. In

England's only innings of 388 for 5 declared Gatting scored 121 and Gower, 131 - his thirteenth Test hundred. Gooch also was asked to bowl again, 4 overs for 15 runs but surely he must have been becoming increasingly bemused by the selection policy of the time; in all six Tests he had opened the batting and had had five different opening partners (Robinson, Slack, Benson, Moxon and Athey). At the end of 1986 only Gatting of the three featured in the top ten first class batting averages – finishing eighth in scoring over 1,000 runs at 54.55. Against New Zealand Gooch had scored 268 runs at 53.60. Gower, deposed as captain had proved his value to England with 293 runs at 58.60 and Captain Gatting had scored just 170 runs at an average of 34.00. He was yet to win a Test as captain.

1986-87
Versus Australia
Gatting's finest hour?

Mike Gatting retained the captaincy for the winter Ashes tour to Australia. Gooch after the trials and tribulations of the West Indies and the summer in England chose not to tour. Many would not blame him but wow, what a tour to miss!
An England side that was famously described as being unable to bat, bowl or field won the Ashes in Australia by two Tests to one. They also swept the board in a hectic round of one-day matches and series against not only Australia but also Pakistan and the West Indies.
It is surely the ultimate irony that these were to be Gatting's only two Test victories as captain, and that Graham Gooch who to this point had played 59 times for England and had scored nearly 3,700 runs at an average of over 37 was not in the side.
Chris Broad had an outstanding tour with the bat and Graham Dilley with the ball. Ian Botham had by his extraordinary standards a modest tour but remained an icon for English cricket at the time. Both Gatting and Gower however had good tours. Gower was second only to Broad in the Test averages with 404

runs at 57.71 and Gatting came in third with 393 runs at 43.66. For Mike Gatting this could be regarded as his finest hour, certainly as England captain. It seems astonishing that in twenty three Tests as captain Gatting was to win only two. And what a two to win, retaining the Ashes and winning in Australia having been so written off as a team and Gatting written off as both captain and player. England won the first Test at Brisbane by 7 wickets with a wonderful century from Botham and 6 wickets from Dilley. Gatting made 61 in England's first innings and Gower 51. The second Test at Perth was Gatting's 50th and was drawn. Gatting celebrated with a 70 in the second innings and Gower with a 'near at his best' 136 was one of three England centurions in the first. The third Test on a flat Adelaide pitch saw Gatting make exactly 100 in England's first innings of 455 replying to Australia's 514 for 5 declared but a duck in the second innings. Over 1,200 runs were scored in the match for just 20 wickets.

England retained the Ashes at Melbourne in the fourth Test in three days; bowling Australia out for 141 and 194 and winning by an innings. Batting at three Gatting scored 40, put on over a hundred with Broad and in doing so passed 3,000 runs in Tests.

England, perhaps a little demob happy lost the last Test at Sydney. Gatting scored 0 and 96, the highest England score in their second innings and Gower made 72 and 37, the highest England score in England's first innings. England also won both of the one-day competitions.

JOB DONE.

1987
Versus Pakistan

So a triumphant Gatting led England in a five Test series against Pakistan and to a world cup in India and Pakistan the following winter. In a summer of poor weather England were held to four draws but were comfortably beaten by an innings at Headingley in the third Test. What should have been a confident England side were however beaten by a Pakistan side inspired by their captain Imran Kahn and batting star Javed Miandad.

England used sixteen players in the series of which five players played in only one Test. Gooch was not one of them. The only batsman to perform for England was captain Gatting who finished with an average of 63.57, with 445 runs and made his highest Test score against Pakistan, his second highest Test score in England of 150 not out which he made at the Oval in the second innings of the fifth Test when England followed on in reply to a mammoth 708 by Pakistan which had included 260 by Miandad, 102 from Salim Malik and 118 by captain Imran Kahn. Gower could average just 29.50 and still no Gooch. Gatting scored 445 runs in the series with an average of 63.57. To his huge credit Gatting also finished third in the first class averages with nearly 1,650 runs at over 60.00. Captaincy it seems did not adversely affect his form!

The World Cup. 1987
No Gower

Oh that reverse sweep!!

England reached the final of the world cup, which had been staged jointly by India and Pakistan. It was not the final that the sub-continent had wanted nor expected with Australia beating Pakistan in their semi-final and England thanks mainly to a magnificent 100 from Gooch beating India in Bombay.

Gooch was back in England colours and had a magnificent tournament. England were captained by Gatting. Gower, in his own words, was feeling tired and jaded and after over 100 one-day internationals had begun to fall out of love with this particular form of the game and so he had made himself unavailable for the winter. After losing the captaincy of both England and Leicestershire, losing 5-0 to the West Indies and sadly losing his mother as well he felt the need for a rest. So firstly Gooch and then Gower had needed a rest. 'Burn out' of front-line first choice England regulars was becoming a serious feature of international cricket and Gatting had found himself without one or the other of the two other G's for a lot of his reign as captain to date. England really should have won, and in chasing an Australian total of 253 fell just 7 runs short. Gatting playing well and on 41 and seemingly guiding England to victory played a reverse sweep to the bowling of his opposing captain, Alan Border, he, rather like Gatting himself was no more than occasional bowler, however Gatting was caught. Australia kept their collective nerve, bowled well at the death and won.

1987-88
Versus Pakistan

So to the winter Test tour against Pakistan – again. Mike Gatting was still captain and this was a tour which I am sure he and most of his players would wish to regret and forget. Tours to Pakistan never had been, never are, and probably never will be easy.
Somehow England undertook this tour with a growing feeling of siege mentality, thinking that they were to be on the wrong end of both the pitches and decisions in the light of Pakistan's disappointment in failing in the world cup. Sadly these feelings became a self-fulfilling prophecy.
The first Test was played at Lahore; much discussion and speculation about the preparation of the wicket to suit the home side, particularly the leg-spin ability of Abdul Qadir – big deal!! England lost this first Test comprehensively. Pakistan won by an innings and 87 runs. England were out batted, out bowled and out fielded by Pakistan. Qadir took 9 of England's first innings wickets for 56 in England's total of 175 all out, four LBW's, and

4 for 45 in the second innings to finish with wonderful match figures of 13-101. Maybe the pitch was under prepared to suit him, maybe the umpiring – remember these were the days before 'neutral' umpires - was not of the highest standard – Shakil Kahn by common consent had an appalling game in just his third Test as an umpire; in Pakistan's only innings there was but one LBW decision (Mudassar Nazar lbw Foster for 120) this by the way was by far the highest score of the Test, whereas England in their two innings of 175 and 130 all out copped 7 LBW's. Maybe this and maybe that, but England lost – badly.

Gooch opened with Chris Broad and made 12 and 15 but is probably best remembered for having to virtually usher Broad off the field in England's second innings when he almost refused to leave the pitch having been given out caught in England's second innings. Gatting made 0 and 23.

No less a tome than Wisden in its report of this Test states:

> "It is one of the tragedies of Test cricket that an epic display of leg spin and googly bowling, which totally dominated the match from it's 11th over, should have occurred in one of the most unsavoury games of cricket ever played. Sadly, the match is doomed to be remembered for its controversies: an under-prepared pitch that proffered an extravagant degree of turn from the start; some appalling umpiring by Shakil Khan; and by Broad's refusal to leave the crease when given out in the second innings."

Sadly the scene had been set for one of the most unpleasant, unsportsmanlike and controversial of all England tours. This is up there with bodyline!

The second Test at Faisalabad was drawn but I doubt if anyone remembers the result. What everybody will remember is the incident when umpire Shakoor Rana accused England captain Mike Gatting of unfair play under law 42 – cheating to you and I – by moving a fielder whilst Eddie Hemmings was running in to bowl. The batsman it is contested, knew what Gatting was doing and the confrontation between Gatting and Rana was unsavory, unnecessary and almost entirely in my opinion the fault of an incompetent umpire with an agenda. The next day's play was lost as Rana demanded an apology from Gatting and England, and the then TCCB, the foreign office and God knows who else became involved. A grudging apology was eventually issued, the match resumed with Pakistan refusing to make up the lost day and, with Pakistan captain Miandad calling his batsman in on the last day with the mandatory last 20 overs yet to start the match was drawn. The irony was that England where in a strong position to win the Test. Gooch, probably dismayed by the whole affair but perhaps relieved to be just playing not captaining made an impressive 65 in England's second innings, Broad perhaps with a point to prove scored his fourth Test hundred and Gatting also perhaps feeling that actions with the bat were most effective made a furious 79 of just 81 balls. Having avoided the cancellation of the tour, which nearly happened, and with diplomatic relations between the two sides virtually non-existent the third Test at Karachi on a good pitch and, with no Rana in a white coat was drawn. Gooch made one of his best scores against Pakistan – 93 – but Gatting failed scoring just 18 and naught.

It is an ironic footnote to this unsavory tour which I am sure everyone particularly the England players were glad to see the back of, that Mike Gatting had made his England debut against Pakistan in Karachi in 1978. He had been dismissed LBW in both innings, in the first innings he scored 5; the bowler was Qadir, the umpire was Shakoor Rana! To end a 'winter of discontent' for English cricket England played a celebratory Test against Australia celebrating 200 hundred years of Australia's white settlement, in January 1987 followed by 3 Tests against New Zealand. The Australia Test was sadly a dour contest ending in a draw.

Against New Zealand all three Tests were also dour draws, rain being a major factor, again there was no Gooch nor Gower. Gatting made 106 runs in 4 innings

1988 v West Indies.
The 3 G's Reunited (ish)

So to England 1988 when England played the West Indies, captained by Richards and with Greenidge, Haynes, Marshall, Ambrose and Walsh in the side. Having lost the previous ten Tests against them and that, at least in part, having caused Gatting's appointment as captain, the G's were at last reunited for the first Test at Trent Bridge. England secured a draw. Gooch played splendidly scoring 73 and 146, in passing 4,000 Test runs, Gower scored an unbeaten 88 in England's second innings and passed 1,000 runs against them which was a major achievement given the dominance and power of the West Indies side of the time but Gatting failed scoring just 5 and 29 batting at 3.

If Mike Gatting had thought that Shakoor Rana and Pakistan had been a problem then he had forgotten about the English tabloid press. His 31st birthday coincided with this Test and stories were sold and emerged regarding the way Gatting may or may not have celebrated this event with a barmaid in his hotel room. The upshot was that Gatting, having survived the appalling events in Pakistan but perhaps having offended the 'Powers' that be who had decided that they must 'back their man' at the time lost the captaincy of his country and decided not make himself available to England for the next Test as a result of a tabloid newspaper story. Having lost the second Test by 134 runs with Gooch scoring 60 runs in the match and Gower 47 runs the 3 G's were reunited for the third Test.

Broad was dropped and Yorkshire's Martin Moxon moved up the order to open with Gooch, and Gatting returned to bat at three. England were comprehensively beaten by an innings, being bowled out for just 93 in their second innings – Marshall 7-22. England scored just 228 runs in the entire Test. Gooch contributed 28 runs, Gatting just 4 and Gower 43 runs. With the weather intervening England had been effectively beaten within three days of actual play. For the 3 G's their own form was poor and they were playing in a side that simply did not seem able to compete. England used 23 players in the series and no less than four different captains. The fourth and fifth Tests were lost equally comprehensively by England. Gatting was dropped for both and Gower missed the fifth Test. For the fifth Test having had Gatting, Emburey and Christopher Cowdrey who therefore followed, uniquely his father as England captain, England were captained by Gooch.. Cowdrey had picked up a foot injury playing for Kent, was not selected for the fifth Test at the Oval Graham Gooch in his 69th Test was given the poisoned chalice of the England captaincy. Gower had captained England, Gatting had captained England now it was the turn of Gooch. He made nearly 100 of England's 407 runs in the match. Neither Gower nor Gatting were selected. England finished the summer with a one-off Test against Sri Lanka – England won, Gooch was captain but still no Gatting nor Gower.

1989
Versus Australia

For a rare occasion England did not tour in the winter. They probably all needed the winter off. But England had been due to tour India and Gooch had been appointed as captain. Low and behold South Africa raised its face again. Objections were raised about some players in the squad. After much wrangling the tour was cancelled. India were also due to host the Commonwealth games that year and there were suggestions that some countries due to send athletes may have threatened to boycott the games. In 1989, having had to deal with Pakistan and Shakoo Rana and then the might of the West Indies, England now had a simple task – an Ashes series against Australia. It was a six Test series and England lost 4-1 – winning only the last meaningless Test. The mantle of captain had now passed back to Gower. Ted Dexter had replaced Peter May as chairman of selectors and a change of captain occurred. There were times during this period of English cricket when one felt that the captaincy was 'awarded,' if that is the word, on the basis of drawing straws and you got the 'honour' on getting the shortest straw. Gower was reappointed as captain although it later emerged that Gatting had been the first choice but that his appointment had been vetoed by some TCCB cricket committee chaired by one Ossie Wheatley.

The three G's played together only once during a long and difficult summer – the second at Lord's. Gatting whose first class season was to end with 1,503 runs at 55.66 with 4 100's and 8 fifties simply could no longer get into the side on a regular basis. England used twenty nine players during the six Tests of the summer and Gatting played but one. In 1989 Gower had scored 1,102 runs at 38.00 with 3 hundreds and 4 fifties and Gooch in the first class season 1980 had scored 1,437 runs at 47.90. He had made only 2 fifties but 6 hundreds. The second Test at Lord's in the summer of 1989 was to be the last time the three G's were to play in the same side for England. In a strange symmetry the three G's had first played together for England at Lord's against Australia in 1980 in the drawn Centenary Test. They scored 167 runs out of 449. In 1989 they scored 245 runs out of England's total of 645 in the match, Gower 57 and 106, Gooch 60 and naught and Gatting 0 and 22. England lost the Test by 6 wickets.

The strain was telling on Gower, he had famously stormed out of the close of play press conference on the Saturday after evening to keep an urgent theatre appointment. But his in the second innings 106 was his fifteenth Test hundred and his seventh against Australia. The first Test at Headingley had been lost by 210 runs. Australia scored 601 for 7 declared having been put in to bat by Gower. Gooch top scored England's second innings with 68. So for the second Test at Gatting's home ground at Lord's the three G's played together for the last time. Australia won by six wickets. England's record against Australia at Lord's is appalling. England last won a Lord's Ashes Test in 1934. Gooch made 60 and 0, Gower had one of his finest Tests as captain scoring 57 and top score of 106 and Gatting 0 and 22. The third Test at Edgbaston was drawn due largely to the weather. England completed their only innings of the match nearly 200 runs behind Australia. Gooch and Gower each made just 8. Gooch bowled in Australia's second innings and took the wicket of Mark Taylor – caught by Botham for 51.

Test number four was played at Manchester and England lost by 9 wickets. The Ashes were back in Australian hands. Equally sad was that at long last after a year of rumour and innuendo, which probably because of his role Gower was about the only player who was almost totally unaware of, the announcement of another rebel tour to South Africa was made. Sixteen names were confirmed, they included Robinson, Emburey and Foster. All of whom where playing in this Test. "Let the mayhem commence" – again! It overshadowed a first ever first class hundred from England wicket-keeper Jack Russell.

The fifth Test was at Trent Bridge and with changes forced on the selectors as much by the South African cricket union as anyone, Mike Atherton and Devon Malcolm debuted. Australia batted first and scored a small matter of 602 for 6 declared.

Marsh and Taylor batted for an entire day and put on a record opening partnership of 329. Gooch had asked to be rested. So Gower was on his own of the three G's. The sixth Test at the Oval, Gooch returned and made 0 and 10 – the rest did not seem to have worked, Gower top scored the first innings with 79 and the match was drawn.

Not Again !
Gatting (SA)

On 1 August 1989, the last day of the fourth Test against Australia at Old Trafford the South African Cricket Union in conjunction with South African Breweries had announced yet another unsanctioned tour to that sad, benighted country. Apartheid was teetering on the brink, long overdue changes were beginning to start and the icon of black resistance to such overt racism, Nelson Mandella, was released after years in prison almost as the plane carrying the rebel touring party landed. Disillusioned, perhaps even angry after recent events or maybe just to put two fingers up to an establishment he may have felt had failed him and a Test career that he judged was ended, and had ended in sad circumstances, the side was captained of all people by Mike Gatting. The Test ban was automatic, inevitable and tragic.

Nearly all the players on this rebel touring side to South Africa had played Test cricket for England and many if not most may have felt that their Test careers were over or close to ending. Gatting was about the only exception to this. With the political events in South Africa unfolding so quickly the tour came to an early end with the players returning home after playing just six matches.

1989/90
Versus The West Indies.

When the touring party for the winter tour to the West Indies was announced with, Gooch as captain there was of course no Gatting, nor, controversially, no Gower. Gower had been on the edge of resigning the captaincy at the end of 1989 but had been effectively sacked anyway. The real shock to him was not to be even in the squad to tour the West Indies. It can only be speculation as to whether his omission from the squad was settled by the selectors with or without the input of the new captain. Remember that at this time the England captain was automatically co-opted onto the selection committee. It should be made clear that for some time now Gower had been suffering from a serious shoulder injury that required surgery. Gower was almost immediately signed up by a national daily newspaper and to join the iconic and magnificent BBC Test Match Special team to report the tour that many felt he should have been playing in. Gower had at this point played 106 Tests averaging 43.43 and had scored 7,383 test runs. He had made 15 100's and 38 50's. Gooch had played 73 Tests he had scored 4,724 runs for England at 36.91. He had made 8 100's and 29 50's.

Gooch, who already had a slightly damaged hand now had his thumb broken by a delivery from Ezra Moseley in the third Test at Trinidad, which was drawn. The second Test scheduled for Bourda had been completely washed out. Lamb took the captaincy for the fourth Test at Barbados and speculation ran rife that the newest recruit to the commentary and press box - Gower could step into the breech. It very nearly happened. In their respective autobiographies both Lamb and Gower make it clear that Gower was being seriously considered to come out of the commentary box and back into the England dressing room.

Gower was approached concerning his fitness and availability to play in the Island match against Barbados. He even had a net or two! And he duly played in the match against Barbados. He was not selected for the Barbados Test, the selectors felt strongly that England should pick from and stick with the original selected squad. And so for the first time in 127 Tests, since February 1978 in Christchurch against New Zealand that none of the three G's played. England lost the Test by 164 runs and the injuries, particularly to the hands of English batsmen continued to pile up. The result was the same in the fifth and final Test. Having started the tour so well with an historic win in Jamaica, lost a Gatting and Gower-less series 2-1 with one draw and the Guyana Test washed out. Although Gower got even closer to playing for England in Antigua. Gower had now left Leicestershire for Hampshire who were on a pre-season tour in the Caribbean, and Gower had played some cricket for Hampshire. The Antigua Test was therefore a deciding Test and Gower was asked again to become available. He was virtually told by England captain Alan Lamb that he would play. Just half an hour before the match he was practicing with England when, finally the decision was made by Gooch and cricket manager Mickey Stewart. No Gower. He was obviously not in the best of form with so little cricket and no-one will ever know how he would have played. The Test match in Antigua was lost by an innings and 32 runs. Greenidge and Haynes put on 298 for the West Indies first innings total of 446. They both made hundreds. England where bowled out for 260 and 154 Rob Bailey was England's top scorer with 42. It is difficult to argue that there was ever an era of the three G's in the sense that the three W's played together and became so eponymous as a trio.

The almost ping pong type selection and captaincy policy of England during the time of the three G's was interesting in that like the three W's they were rarely in competition with each other for a place in the side and yet, unlike the three W's, they so rarely played together. Of course it must be said that England have always had a far greater pool of players to choose from and that therefore competition was always fiercer. Also of course both Gooch and Gatting incurred Test bans with unsanctioned tours to South Africa.

It seemed that by the end of this tour, if not at the start, the Test careers of Gower and Gatting were effectively over. In fact both players were to represent their country again but never together.

1990
Versus New Zealand and India

Gooch was to captain England for another thirty Tests of which Gower played ten and dear old Gatting just four. In 1990 England played three Tests against New Zealand in which England, captained again by Gooch, won and three Tests against India. Gooch scored his mammoth 333 at Lord's in the first innings of the series; finishing with over 750 runs in six innings at an average of over 125. Gower was recalled and joined in the fun of a series victory scoring over 290 runs at an average in excess of 72, finishing the last Test with 157 not out.

1990-91
Versus Australia.

Gower was included in the squad for the Ashes tour to Australia. England had a bad tour losing the series 3 Tests to nil and in one incident the extraordinary differences between the approach of these two fine players was to be set in stone – or perhaps water!.
Gower played all five Tests. He passed 8,000 runs for England in the second innings of the third Test at Sydney. He scored two hundreds sandwiched between them was his first duck for England in 119 innings. He ended the tour with over 400 runs at 45.22, a severe reprimand and a £1,000 fine! During a fairly meaningless game at Carrara Gower's frustration with the somewhat 'all play and practice' regime of the tour and his innate mischievousness got the better of him and he hired an old bi-plane from an airfield next door. He duly 'buzzed' the ground at very low level where Alan Lamb and Robin Smith where batting.
Gower was actually playing in the game and John Morris a far less established England player but who had scored a hundred had gleefully joined in the airborne jaunt.
Graham Gooch utterly dedicated, determined and committed to England. David Gower utterly dedicated, determined and committed to England. Gower had played over 100 times for England, he had scored over 8,000 runs for England, and had captained his country. Gooch had played over 80 times for England he had scored over 6,000 runs and was England captain.
Gooch convinced that fitness, practice, training and total focus on playing cricket was why you where on tour and the best way to bring out the best in you as an England Test cricketer. Gower convinced that there always had to be a time for 'R & R' and that there had to be an element of fun in the game to bring out the best in you as an England Test cricketer. You decide!
Gooch had missed the first Test for yet more surgery to his hand. None-the-less he scored over 400 runs and averaged well over 50.00.

1991 - 1992
Versus West Indies. Sri Lanka. New Zealand

England played a 5 match series against the West Indies and a one-off Test against Sri Lanka. Gooch was captain. Gower did not play, Gatting still banned. The series was drawn two Tests each, and England then beat Sri Lanka. England awarded five new caps. A new generation was emerging. Gooch scored nearly 700 runs, including 2 centuries.

Gooch led England in the winter for 3 Tests against New Zealand, which England won 2-0, the last Test at Wellington was drawn. Gooch passed 7,000 runs for England during the series.

1992
Versus Pakistan
Goodbye Gower

The fair haired left-handed England warrior returned for one last tilt. This time against the in swinging windmills of Waqar Younis and Wasim Akram! Pakistan played a five Tests series in England. Waqar Younis and Wasim Akram were in their pomp with high pace late swinging deliveries. After a rain ruined draw at Edgbaston England had been beaten in a thrilling Test at Lord's and for the third Test at Old Trafford David Gower was recalled for his 115th Test – a record – and passed the record aggregate run total for England – 8,114 runs, previously held by Boycott. Gower's score of 73 in England's only innings was only surpassed by Gooch with 78. The Test was drawn.

England won at Headingley by 6 wickets. Gooch scored 135 in the first innings, his first against Pakistan. Gower got another first in being not out for his first time in both innings of a Test. England had slumped from 292 for 3 to 320 all out – 28 runs for 7 wickets, leaving Gower 18 not out. In what was to be Gower's last Test England were beaten by 10 wickets at the Oval. With Akram taking 9 wickets in the match and Younis 6 wickets Gower scored 27 and 1. Gooch made 20 and 24. Gower had already decided on his retirement from cricket. The 'daily grind' of county cricket had never really appealed to him and he was increasingly at odds with the way International cricket, particularly with one-day cricket so prevalent, was becoming. David Gower was never going to be at ease with the treadmill – be it in the gym or on the field! He never played for England again.

1992-93
Versus India
Hello Gatting

England toured India, the scene of some of Gatting's finest times for England. He was recalled for the tour having missed thirty three Tests as punishment for leading the unofficial tour to South Africa. So the 'no nonsense' square jawed street fighter returned for the gifted curly-haired left handed Gower. India won the first Test at Calcutta by 8 wickets. England were bowled out for just 163 and 286 but Gatting celebrated his recall by top scoring in both innings – 33 and 81. Gooch made just 35 in the match. Gooch missed the next Test unwell. Stewart captained, Gatting scored just 21 runs and England lost by an innings. Gatting however passed 4,000 Test runs. Things did not get any better for the third Test. India won by an innings again. England's lack of technique against class spinners was being cruelly exposed. Gatting however was doing his best to reaffirm what a good player of spin he could be. He made 61 in the second innings – his 20th 50 for England. So England lost by three Tests to nil. England also lost a one-off Test against Sri Lanka. Gooch did not play. Gatting batted at three and made just 29 and 18.

1993
Versus Australia.

Australia came to England for six Tests. They won the series. England won only the last Test at the Oval. They drew only one and lost the other four. After the fourth Test at Headingley Gooch resigned the captaincy. Captained by Border the Australians included the Waugh twins, Mark Taylor, Boon, Slater, Healey and a certain Shane Warne. Gatting played only the first two Tests and yes everybody remembers that first Warne ball in England and yes it was Gatting he bowled. Enough said! Gatting however scored 59 in the second innings of the second Test and yes he was victim to Warne again, but England still lost and Gatting was dropped for the rest of the series. England used twenty four players and awarded seven new caps in the series Despite the traumas of his season Gooch played all six Tests, he scored over 670 runs at an average of over 50 including 2 hundreds and 4 fifties. He also passed Gower's total of 8,231 England Test runs when he reached 18 in the final England innings of the series. England toured the West Indies in 1993-94 but neither Gooch nor Gatting went. England lost the series by three Tests to one.

1994
Versus New Zealand & South Africa

In 1994 Gooch returned to the side for the three Test series against New Zealand, followed by three Tests against ironically the now forgiven and re-instated South Africa. Against New Zealand he scored his second highest Test score of 210 in the first Test at Trent Bridge. England won the series and Gooch scored only another 13 runs in the remaining two Tests, he made 2 ducks. Against his nemesis South Africa, in three tests, he could only manage 139 runs with a top score of 33; the series was drawn one Test each.

The End

In 1994/95 Gooch toured Australia, and Mike Gatting, having finished the English summer with an amazing 1,671 runs scored in just 19 innings with a top score of 225 runs at an average of 69.62 could simply not be ignored by England and was recalled to join Gooch on tour. They played together in all five Tests and both announced their retirement from Test cricket prior to the last Test at Perth. Atherton was the England captain and in the first Test at Brisbane Australia won again, by 184 runs. Gooch batted at 5 and Gatting at 6 and in a strong batting line up England were bowled out for just 167. In the second innings Gooch made 56 and Gatting made just 23 runs in the match. Australia won easily again at Melbourne by 295 runs. Boon scored 131 in Australia's second innings and Warne took 9 wickets in the match for 80 runs. Gooch scored 17 and Gatting 34 runs in the Test. The third Test at Sydney was affected by rain but England at one stage were in a position to win having bowled Australia out for 116 in their first innings; Gough 6-49. Atherton in pursuit of victory made a hard decision, he declared England's first innings at 255 for 2 with Hick on 98 not out. The Test was drawn.

Despite the usual mounting England injury list, they won in Adelaide by 106 runs. Gooch scored 81 runs in the match and Gatting his 10th and last hundred for England – 117. Australia were comfortable victors in the final Test at Perth. Gooch passed Gower's record of 117 Tests. In their last innings Gooch was caught and bowled for 4 and Gatting bowled for 8. England were all out for 123 and at one stage where 27 for 6. And so it ended with something of a whimper.

Both men had served English cricket well and continued so to do; both served as England selectors and county coaches; Gower went for the commentators shilling!

The Captains G.

I sincerely believe that all three of these very, very fine players were somewhat reluctant captains appointed in panic when there seemed to be no alternative. All three could and should have played together more often, but at least in part, with Gooch and Gatting both incurring bans for unofficial tours to the sports isolated South Africa, it was never meant to be.

In 1964 the film Zulu was released and I find my self thinking of Gower as the seemingly effete officer who underneath cares very much and is as tough as he needs to be, Gooch the absolute professional sergeant major, dedicated and showing always the tough love ensuring his men were as well prepared as possible and Gatting equally tough and belligerent, no political animal taking a word as a bond and not suffering fools gladly as the utterly committed NCO who would be the first 'over the top', knowing that by sheer example his men would follow, and that no fools either above or below him in rank would be tolerated lightly. All three were of the "all for one and one for all" mentality.

All three, however reluctantly, captained England; Gatting captained England on twenty three occasions but only five times did Gooch and Gower play with him as captain. Similarly during Gower's times as captain, a total of thirty two occasions, he only had both Gooch and Gatting in the same side nine times. Gooch was to lead England thirty four times but was never to lead both Gower and Gatting in the same side.

Fantasy time

Imagine a side with these six players: Worrell, Walcott, Weekes, Gooch, Gatting, Gower.

Well that would seem to take care of the batting. Depending on the state of Walcott's back we will need a wicket-keeper, and if we set a rule of only players from the two eras and from the two countries: my choice for his sheer ability with the gloves would be Bob Taylor.

Bowlers: Ramadhin and Valentine to spin it a bit and as some pace to back up to Worrell; my choice would be Malcolm Marshall. I fancy if you asked Gatting, Gooch or Gower they would not be too dismayed to have Malcolm Marshall on their side for a change!

If only for the sake of fairness and balance I would be strongly tempted to throw one I T Botham into the mix. At least in would be a lively and interesting dressing-room. As for Captain? It could be argued that with that team you would hardly need one. But I think I will give it to Gooch if only to close the circle in that he will then have captained both Gower and Gatting at the same time.

Batting order: Gooch (capt), Worrell, Weekes, Gower, Walcott, Gatting, Botham, Marshall, Taylor (wkt), Ramadhin and Valentine.

I might be tempted to ask Gary Sobers to cover. After all, apart from perhaps Taylor he could easily take the place and fill the roll of all and any of the other ten.

THE STATISTICS.

Player Profiles: Worrell, Weekes, Walcott

Sir Frank M M Worrell   1924-1967
Right Hand Bat   Left Arm fast medium bowler.
Wisden Cricketer of the year – 1951
Knighted – 1964
Main Teams: West Indies. Barbados. Jamaica.
Test Debut: V England 1948 – Port-of-Spain
Last Test: V England 1963 – The Oval
Test caps: 51 - 15 as captain.
First Class career: 1941-42 to 1963-64

Sir Everton de Courcy Weekes.   1925-
Right Hand Bat.   Right Arm Leg Break bowler.
Wisden Cricketer of the year – 1951
Knighted – 1995
Main Teams: West Indies. Barbados
Test Debut: V England 1948 - Bridgetown
Last Test: V Pakistan 1958 – Port-of-Spain
Test Caps: 48
First Class career: 1944-45 to 1963-64
Other: Coach. ICC match referee.

Sir Clyde L Walcott   1926- 2006
Right Hand Bat   Right Arm Bowler
Wicket Keeper.
Wisden Cricketer of the year – 1958
OBE – 1966 Knighted – 1994
Main Teams: West Indies. Barbados. Guiana.
Test Debut: V England 1948 - Bridgetowm
Last Test: V England 1960 - Port-of-Spain
Test Caps: 44
First Class career: 1941-42 to 1963-64
Other: West Indies selector. Manager of West Indies teams 1975-79 & 1987. ICC match referee. Chairman ICC.

Player profiles: Gooch, Gatting, Gower.

Graham H Gooch　　　Born: 1953
Right Hand Bat　　　Right Arm bowler
Wisden Cricketer of the year – 1980
Main Teams: England. Essex. Western Province.
Test Debut: V Australia 1975 - Edgbaston
Last Test:　V Australia 1995 – Perth
Test Caps: 118
First Class career: 1973- 1997
Other: Coach. England selector

Michael W Gatting　　　Born: 1957
Right Hand Bat　　　Right Arm Bowler.
Wisden Cricketer of the year – 1984
Main Teams: England. Middlesex.
Test Debut: V Pakistan 1978 - Karachi
Last Test:　V Australia 1995 – Perth
Test Caps: 79
First Class career: 1975-1988
Other: Coach. England selector.

David I Gower　　　Born: 1957
Left Hand Bat　　　Right Arm Bowler.
Wisden Cricketer of the Year: 1979
Main Teams: England. Leicestershire. Hampshire.
Test Debut: V Pakistan 1978 – Edgbaston
Last Test:　V Pakistan 1992 – The Oval
Test Caps: 117
First Class career: 1975-1993
Other: Commentator

Overall Records:
Worrell. Weekes. Walcott

Worrell:
Batting:

	M.	Inns	NO	Runs	HS	Ave	100	50	Ct	St
Test:	51	87	9	3860	261	49.48	9	22	43	0
F/C:	208	326	49	15025	308*	54.24	39	80	139	0

Bowling:

	M.	Balls	Runs	Wkts	bb	Ave	econ
Test:	51	7141	2672	69	7-70	38.72	2.24
F/C:	208	26740	10115	349	7-70	28.98	2.26

Weekes:
Batting:

	M.	Inns	NO	Runs	HS	Ave	100	50	Ct	St
Test:	48	81	5	4455	207	58.61	15	19	49	0
F/C:	152	241	24	12010	304*	55.34	36	54	124	1

Bowling:

	M.	Balls	Runs	Wkts	bb	Ave	econ
Test:	48	122	77	1	1-8	77.00	3.78
F/C:	152	1125	731	17	4-38	43.00	3.89

Walcott:
Batting:

	M.	Inns	NO	Runs	HS	Ave	100	50	Ct	St
Test:	44	74	7	3798	220	56.68	15	14	53	11
F/C:	146	238	29	11820	314*	56.55	40	54	174	33

Bowling:

	M.	Balls	Runs	Wkts	bb	Ave	econ
Test:	44	1194	408	11	3-50	37.09	2.05
F/C:	146	3449	1269	35	5-41	36.25	2.20

Worrell Test Record: Batting

Year	V	M	Inns	NO	Runs	HS	Ave	100	50	Ct	St
1947-48	Eng	3	4	2	294	131*	147.00	1	1	2	
1950	Eng	4	6	0	539	261	89.83	2	1	4	
1951-52	Aus	5	10	0	337	108	33.70	1	1	4	
1951-52	NZ	2	3	1	233	100	116.50	1	2	2	
1952-53	Ind	5	8	0	398	237	49.75	1	1	8	
1953-54	Eng	4	8	1	334	167	47.71	1	2	4	
1954-55	Aus	4	8	0	206	61	25.75	0	2	2	
1957	Eng	5	10	1	350	191*	38.88	1	1	1	
1959-60	Eng	4	6	1	320	197*	64.00	1	1	4	
1960-61	Aus	5	10	0	375	82	37.50	0	5	2	
1961-62	Ind	5	6	2	332	98*	83.00	0	4	7	
1963	Eng	5	8	1	142	74*	20.28	0	1	3	
Totals:		51	87	9	3860	261	49.49	9	22	43	
Country	Eng	25	42	6	1979	261	54.97	6	7	18	
	Aust	14	28	0	918	108	32.78	1	8	8	
	Ind	10	14	2	730	237	60.83	1	5	15	
	NZ	2	3	1	233	100	116.50	1	2	2	
Home		25	40	6	1884	237	55.41	4	11	27	
Away		26	47	3	1976	261	44.91	5	11	16	

Worrell Test Record: Bowling

Year	V	Balls	Mdn	Runs	Wkts	Ave	bb
1947-48	Eng	420	10	156	1	156.00	1-55
1950	Eng	590	36	182	6	30.33	3-40
1951-52	Aus	713	10	329	17	19.35	6-38
1951-52	NZ	282	14	81	2	40.50	1-20
1952-53	Ind	810	35	262	7	37.42	2-32
1953-54	Eng	414	9	193	2	96.50	1-29
1954-55	Aus	690	23	311	3	103.66	2-120
1957	Eng	770	25	343	10	34.30	7-70
1959-60	Eng	695	37	233	6	38.83	4-49
1960-61	Aus	1072	34	357	10	35.70	3-27
1961-62	Ind	415	25	121	2	60.50	2-12
1963	Eng	270	16	104	3	34.66	2-12
Totals:		7141	274	2672	69	38.72	7-70
Country	Eng	3159	133	1211	28	43.25	7-70
	Aust	2475	67	997	30	33.23	6-38
	Ind	1225	60	383	9	42.55	2-12
	NZ	282	14	81	2	40.50	1-20
Home		3444	139	1276	21	60.76	
Away		3697	135	1396	48	29.08	

Weekes Test record: Batting

Year	V	M	Inns	NO	Runs	HS	Ave	100	50	Ct	St
1947-48	Eng	4	6	0	293	141	48.83	1	0	1	
1948-49	Ind	5	7	0	779	194	111.28	4	2	1	
1950	Eng	4	6	0	338	129	56.33	1	3	11	
1951-52	Aust	5	10	0	245	70	24.50	0	2	5	
1951-52	NZ	2	3	0	60	51	20.00	0	1	2	
1952-53	Ind	5	8	1	716	207	102.28	3	2	9	
1953-54	Eng	4	8	1	487	206	69.57	1	3	3	
1954-55	Aust	5	10	2	469	139	58.62	1	3	3	
1955-56	NZ	4	5	0	418	156	83.60	3	0	5	
1957	Eng	5	10	0	195	90	19.50	0	1	4	
1957-58	Pak	5	8	1	455	197	65.00	1	2	5	
Totals:			48	81	5	4455	207		15	19	49
Country	Eng	17	30	1	1313	206	45.27	3	7	19	
	Aust	10	20	2	714	139	39.66	1	5	8	
	Ind	10	15	1	1495	207	106.78	7	4	10	
	NZ	6	8	0	478	156	59.75	3	1	7	
	Pak	5	8	1	455	197	65.00	1	2	5	
Home		23	40	5	2420	207	69.14	7	10	21	
Away		25	41	0	2035	194	49.63	8	9	28	

Weekes Test Record. Bowling:

Year	V	Balls	Mdn	Runs	Wkts	Ave	BB
1947-48	Eng						
1948-49	Ind	12	0	5	0		
1950	Eng						
1951-52	Aust						
1951-52	NZ						
1952-53	Ind	18	0	11	0		
1953-54	Eng	42	1	39	0		
1954-55	Aust	14	0	8	1	8.00	1-8
1955-56	NZ						
1957	Eng						
1957-58	Pak	36	2	14	0		
Totals:		122	3	77	1	77.00	
Country	Eng	42	1	39	0		
	Aust	14	0	8	1	8.00	
	Ind	30	0	16	0		
	NZ						
	Pak	36	2	14	0		
Home		110	3	72	1	72.00	
Away		12	0	5	0		

Walcott Test Record. Batting:

Year	V	M	Inns	NO	Runs	HS	Ave	100	50	Ct	St
1947-48	Eng	4	7	1	133	45	22.16	0	0	11	5
1948-49	Ind	5	7	0	452	152	64.57	2	2	9	2
1950	Eng	4	6	1	229	168*	45.80	1	0	4	3
1951-52	Aus	3	6	0	87	60	14.50	0	1	4	1
1951-52	NZ	2	3	0	199	115	66.33	1	1	2	
1952-53	Ind	5	7	1	457	125	76.16	2	1	6	
1953-54	Eng	5	10	2	698	220	87.25	3	3	3	
1954-55	Aus	5	10	0	827	155	82.70	5	2	5	
1957	Eng	5	10	1	247	90	27.44	0	1	4	
1957-58	Pak	4	5	1	385	145	96.25	1	2	3	
1959-60	Eng	2	3	0	84	53	28.00	0	1	2	
Totals:		44	74	7	3798	220	56.68	15	14	53	11
Country	Eng	20	36	5	1391	220	44.87	4	5	24	8
	Ind	10	14	1	909	152	69.92	4	3	15	2
	Aus	8	16	0	914	155	57.12	5	3	9	1
	Pak	4	5	1	385	145	96.25	1	2	3	
	NZ	2	3	0	199	115	66.33	1	1	2	
Home		25	42	5	2584	220	69.84	11	9	30	5
Away		19	32	2	1214	168*	40.47	4	5	23	6

Walcott Test Record. Bowling:

Year	V	Balls	Mdn	Runs	Wkt	Ave	BB
1947-48	Eng						
1948-49	Ind	18	0	12	0		
1950	Eng	24	1	12	0		
1951-52	Aus						
1951-52	NZ						
1952-53	Ind	210	14	48	2	24.00	2-12
1953-54	Eng	318	24	94	4	23.50	3-52
1954-55	Aus	426	24	152	4	38.00	3-50
1957	Eng	6	0	4	0		
1957-58	Pak	72	5	16	0		
1959-60	Eng	120	4	70	1	70.00	1-43
Totals:		1194	72	408	11	37.09	3-50
Country	Eng	468	29	180	5	36.00	3-52
	Ind	228	14	60	2	30.00	2-12
	Aus	426	24	152	4	38.00	3-50
	Pak	72	5	16	0		
	NZ						
Home		1146	71	380	11	34.55	3-50
Away		48	1	28	0		

All 3 W's when playing together.
Batting:

Country	M	Name	Inns	No	Runs	HS	Ave
Eng	15	Worrell	26	3	1441	261	62.65
		Weekes	26	0	1108	206	42.62
		Walcott	27	4	956	168*	41.57
Aust	7	Worrell	14	0	371	64	26.50
		Weekes	14	1	430	81	33.08
		Walcott	14	0	678	155	48.43
Ind	5	Worrell	8	0	398	237	49.75
		Weekes	8	1	716	207	102.29
		Walcott	7	1	457	125	76.17
NZ	2	Worrell	3	1	233	100	116.50
		Weekes	3	0	60	51	20.00
		Walcott	3	0	199	115	66.33
Totals:	29		153	11	7047		
Results:							
			Won	Lost	Drew		

All 3 W's when playing together..
Bowling:

Country	M	Name	Balls	Mdn	Runs	Wkts	Ave	BB
Eng	15	Worrell	1816	70	755	18	41.94	7-70
		Weekes	42	1	39	0		
		Walcott	300	23	90	4	22.50	3-52
Aust	7	Worrell	736	27	555	13	42.69	4-95
		Weekes	14	0	8	1	8.00	1-8
		Walcott	312	19	107	3	35.67	3-50
Ind	5	Worrell	810	35	262	7	37.43	2-32
		Weekes	18	0	11	0		
		Walcott	210	14	48	2	24.00	2-12
NZ	2	Worrell	282	14	81	2	40.50	1-20
		Weekes						
		Walcott						
Totals:	29		4540	203	1956	50		
Results:								
			Won	Lost	Drew			
			7	12	10			

Overall Records:
Gooch. Gower. Gatting.

Gooch
Batting:

	M.	Inns	NO	Runs	HS	Ave	100	50	Ct	St
Test:	118	215	6	8900	333	42.58	20	46	103	0
F/C:	581	990	75	44846	333	49.01	128	217	555	0

Bowling:

	M.	Balls	Runs	Wkts	bb	Ave	econ
Test:	118	2655	1069	23	3-39	46.47	2.41
F/C:	581	18785	8457	246	7-14	34.37	2.70

Gower
Batting:

	M.	Inns	NO	Runs	HS	Ave	100	50	Ct	St
Test:	117	204	18	8231	215	44.25	18	39	74	0
F/C:	448	727	70	26339	228	40.08	53	136	280	1

Bowling:

	M.	Balls	Runs	Wkts	bb	Ave	econ
Test:	117	36	20	1	1-1	20.00	3.33
F/C:	448	260	227	4	3-47	56.75	5.23

Gatting:
Batting:

	M.	Inns	NO	Runs	HS	Ave	100	50	Ct	St
Test:	79	138	14	4409	207	35.55	10	21	59	0
F/C:	551	861	123	36549	258	49.52		94	181	493

Bowling:

	M.	Balls	Runs	Wkts	bb	Ave	econ
Test:	79	752	317	4	1-14	79.25	2.52
F/C:	551	10061	4703	158	5-34	29.76	2.80

Gooch Test Records. Batting

Year	V	M	Inns	NO	Runs	HS	Ave	100	50	Ct	St
1975	Aus	2	4	0	37	31	9.25	0	0	2	
1978	Pak	2	2	0	74	54	37.00	0	1	2	
1978	NZ	3	5	2	190	91*	63.33	0	2	1	
1978-79	Aus	6	11	0	246	74	22.36	0	1	9	
1979	Ind	4	5	0	207	83	41.40	0	2	6	
1979-80	Aus	2	4	0	172	99	43.00	0	2	1	
1979-80	Ind	1	2	1	57	49*	57.00	0	0	1	
1980	WI	5	10	0	394	123	39.40	1	2	5	
1980	Aus	1	2	0	24	16	12.00	0	0	0	
1980-81	WI	4	8	0	460	153	57.50	2	1	3	
1981	Aus	5	10	0	139	44	13.90	0	0	1	
1981-82	Ind	6	10	1	487	127	54.11	1	4	4	
1981-82	SL	1	2	0	53	31	26.50	0	0	1	
1985	Aus	6	9	0	487	196	54.11	1	2	4	
1985-86	WI	5	10	0	276	53	27.60	0	4	6	
1986	Ind	3	6	0	175	114	29.16	1	0	5	
1986	NZ	3	5	0	268	183	53.60	1	0	6	
1987-88	Pak	3	6	0	225	93	37.50	0	2	3	
1988	WI	5	10	0	459	146	45.90	1	3	6	
1988	SL	1	2	0	111	75	55.50	0	1	3	
1989	Aus	5	9	0	183	68	20.33	0	2	4	
1989-90	WI	2	4	1	128	84	42.66	0	1	2	
1990	NZ	3	5	0	306	154	61.20	1	1	3	
1990	Ind	3	6	0	752	333	125.33	3	2	4	
1990-91	Aus	4	8	0	426	117	53.25	1	4	6	
1991	WI	5	9	1	480	154*	60.00	1	2	6	
1991	SL	1	2	0	212	174	106.00	1	0	0	
1991-92	NZ	3	5	0	161	114	32.20	1	0	0	
1992	Pak	5	8	0	384	135	48.00	1	2	2	

Gooch Test Record: Batting Cont:

Year	V	M	Inns	NO	Runs	HS	Ave	100	50	Ct	St
1992-93	Ind	2	4	0	47	18	11.75	0	0	1	
1993	Aus	6	12	0	673	133	56.08	2	4	2	
1994	NZ	3	4	0	223	210	55.75	1	0	3	
1994	SA	3	6	0	139	33	23.16	0	0	1	
1994-95	Aus	5	10	0	245	56	24.50	0	1	0	
Totals:		118	215	6	8900	333	42.58	120	96	103	0
Country	Aus	42	79	0	2632	196	33.31	4	16	29	
	WI	26	51	2	2197	154*	44.83	5	13	28	
	Ind	19	33	2	1725	333	55.64	5	8	21	
	NZ	15	24	2	1148	210	52.18	4	3	13	
	Pak	10	16	0	683	135	42.68	1	5	7	
	SL	3	6	0	376	174	62.66	1	1	4	
	SA	3	6	0	139	33	23.16	0	0	1	
Home		74	131	3	5917	333	46.23	15	26	66	0
Away		44	84	3	2983	153	36.83	5	20	37	0

Gooch Test Record: Bowling:

Year	V	Balls	Mdn	Runs	Wkt	Ave	BB
1975	Aus						
1978	Pak						
1978	NZ	60	0	29	0		
1978-79	Aus	48	1	15	0		
1979	Ind	150	9	49	1	49.00	1-16
1979-80	Aus	114	6	36	2	18.00	2-16
1979-80	Ind	24	2	3	0		
1980	WI	150	7	59	3	19.66	2-18
1980	Aus	48	3	16	0		
1980-81	WI	84	5	36	0		
1981	Aus	60	4	28	0		
1981-82	Ind	199	6	77	2	38.50	2-12
1981-82	SL						
1985	Aus	248	10	102	2	51.00	2-57
1985-86	WI	42	3	27	1	27.00	1-21
1986	Ind	78	2	31	1	31.00	1-19
1986	NZ	114	9	38	1	38.00	1-23
1987-88	Pak	12	1	4	0		
1988	WI						
1988	SL						
1989	Aus	186	9	72	1	72.00	1-30
1989-90	WI						
1990	NZ	78	7	25	0		
1990	Ind	108	4	70	1	70.00	1-26
1990-91	Aus	138	5	69	2	34.50	1-23
1991	WI	48	1	14	0		
1991	SL						
1991-92	NZ						
1992	Pak	306	15	94	5	18.80	3-39

Gooch Test Record. Bowling: Cont.

Year	V	Balls	Mdn	Runs	Wkt	Ave	BB
1992-93	Ind						
1993	Aus	150	6	66	0		
1994	NZ	42	1	26	0		
1994	SA	18	0	9	0		
1994-95	Aus	150	6	74	1	74.00	1-20
Totals:		2655	122	1069	23	46.48	3-39
Country	Aus	1142	50	478	8	59.75	2-16
	WI	324	16	136	4	34.00	2-18
	Ind	559	23	230	5	46.00	2-12
	NZ	294	17	118	1	118.00	1-23
	Pak	318	16	98	5	19.60	3-39
	SL						
	SA	18	0	9	0		
Home		1844	87	728	15	48.53	
Away		811	35	341	8	42.62	

Gower Test Records. Batting:

Year	V	M	Inns	NO	Runs	HS	Ave	100	50	Ct
1978	Pak	3	3	0	153	58	51.00	0	2	0
1978	NZ	3	5	0	285	111	57.00	1	1	0
1978-79	Aus	6	11	1	420	102	42.00	1	1	4
1979	Ind	4	5	1	289	200*	72.25	1	1	2
1979-80	Aus	3	6	1	152	98*	30.40	0	1	3
1979-80	Ind	1	1	0	16	16	16.00	0	0	0
1980	WI	1	2	0	21	20	10.50	0	0	1
1980	Aus	1	2	0	80	45	40.00	0	0	0
1980-81	WI	4	8	1	376	154*	53.71	1	1	2
1981	Aus	5	10	0	250	89	25.00	0	1	3
1981-82	Ind	6	9	1	375	85	46.87	0	4	1
1981-82	SL	1	2	1	131	89	131.00	0	1	4
1982	Ind	3	5	1	152	47	38.00	0	0	2
1982	Pak	3	6	0	197	74	32.83	0	2	2
1982-83	Aus	5	10	0	441	114	44.10	1	3	4
1983	NZ	4	8	1	404	112*	57.71	2	1	6
1983-84	NZ	3	4	0	69	33	17.25	0	0	2
1983-84	Pak	3	5	1	449	173*	112.25	2	2	3
1984	WI	5	10	1	171	57*	19.00	0	1	3
1984	SL	1	1	0	55	55	55.00	0	1	1
1984-85	Ind	5	7	1	167	78	27.83	0	1	6
1985	Aus	6	9	0	732	215	81.33	3	1	6
1985-86	WI	5	10	0	370	90	37.00	0	3	3
1986	Ind	2	4	0	101	49	25.25	0	0	2
1986	NZ	3	5	0	293	131	58.60	1	2	3
1986-87	Aus	5	8	1	404	136	57.71	1	2	1
1987	Pak	5	8	0	236	61	29.50	0	2	2

Gower Test Record. Batting Cont

Year	V	M	Inns	NO	Runs	HS	Ave	100	50	Ct
1988	WI	4	8	1	211	88*	30.14	0	1	2
1989	Aus	6	11	0	383	106	34.81	0	1	2
1990	Ind	3	6	2	291	157*	72.75	1	0	0
1990-91	Aus	5	10	1	407	123	45.22	2	1	1
1992	Pak	3	5	2	150	73	50.00	0	1	1
Totals:		117	204	18	8231	215	44.25	117	88	72
Country										
	Aus	42	77	4	3269	215	44.78	9	12	26
	Ind	24	37	6	1391	200*	44.87	2	6	13
	WI	19	38	3	1149	154*	32.82	1	6	11
	Pak	17	27	3	1185	173*	49.37	2	9	8
	NZ	13	22	1	1051	131	50.04	4	4	11
	SL	2	3	1	186	89	93.00	0	2	5
Home		65	113	9	4454			9	18	38
Away		52	91	9	3777			8	20	34

Bowling:

Gower bowled 36 balls in Tests:
12 balls taking 1wkt for 2 runs V. India in 1981-82
6 balls for 5 runs V. New Zealand in 1986
18 balls for 13 runs V. India in 1984-85

Gatting Test Record. Batting:

Year	V	M	inns	NO	Runs	HS	Ave	100	50	Ct
1977-78	Pak	1	2	0	11	6	5.50	0	0	2
1977-78	NZ	1	1	0	0	0	0.00	0	0	1
1980	WI	4	7	0	172	56	24.57	0	1	1
1980	Aus	1	2	1	63	51*	63.00	0	1	1
1980-81	WI	1	2	0	2	2	1.00	0	0	1
1981	Aus	6	12	0	370	59	30.83	0	4	8
1981-82	Ind	5	6	1	68	32	13.60	0	0	0
1982	Pak	3	6	1	111	32*	22.20	0	0	3
1983	NZ	2	4	0	121	81	30.25	0	1	4
1983-84	NZ	2	3	1	38	19*	19.00	0	0	2
1983-84	Pak	3	5	0	158	75	31.60	0	2	6
1984	WI	1	2	0	30	29	15.00	0	0	2
1984-85	Ind	5	9	3	575	207	95.83	2	1	4
1985	Aus	6	9	3	527	160	87.83	2	3	0
1985-86	WI	1	2	0	16	15	8.00	0	0	2
1986	Ind	3	6	2	293	183*	73.25	1	0	3
1986	NZ	3	5	0	170	121	34.00	1	0	2
1986-87	Aus	5	9	0	393	100	43.66	1	3	5
1987	Pak	5	8	1	445	150*	63.57	2	1	2

Gatting Test Record. Batting: Cont.

Year	V	M	inns	NO	Runs	HS	Ave	100	50	Ct
1987-88	Pak	3	6	0	128	79	21.33	0	1	1
1987-88	Aus	1	1	0	13	13	13.00	0	0	0
1987-88	NZ	3	4	1	106	42	35.33	0	0	0
1988	WI	2	4	0	38	29	9.50	0	0	1
1989	Aus	1	2	0	22	22	11.00	0	0	0
1992-93	Ind	3	6	0	219	81	36.50	0	2	1
1992-93	SL	1	2	0	47	29	23.50	0	0	2
1993	Aus	2	4	0	91	59	22.75	0	1	2
1994-95	Aus	5	9	0	182	117	20.22	1	0	3
Totals:		79	138	14	4409	207	35.55	110	71	59
Country	Aus	27	48	4	1661	160	37.75	4	12	19
	Ind	16	27	6	1155	207	55.00	3	3	8
	Pak	15	27	2	853	150*	34.12	2	4	14
	NZ	11	17	2	435	121	29.00	1	1	9
	WI	9	17	0	258	56	15.17	0	1	7
	SL	1	2	0	47	29	23.50	0	0	2
Home		39	71	8	2453	183*	32.06	6	12	29
Away		40	67	6	1956	207	32.06	4	9	30

Gatting Test Record. Bowling:

Year	V	Balls	Mdn	Runs	Wkt	Ave	BB
1977-78	Pak						
1977-78	NZ	8	0	1	0		
1980	WI						
1980	Aus						
1980-81	WI						
1981	Aus	18	1	13	0		
1981-82	Ind	6	0	4	0		
1982	Pak	60	3	21	0		
1983	NZ	42	3	13	0		
1983-84	NZ	60	4	28	1	28.00	1-14
1983-84	Pak	30	0	35	1	35.00	1-17
1984	WI						
1984-85	Ind	78	1	36	0		
1985	Aus	30	0	16	0		
1985-86	WI						
1986	Ind	12	0	10	0		
1986	NZ						
1986-87	Aus	138	7	39	0		
1987	Pak	132	5	40	0		

Gatting Test Record: Bowling Cont

Year	V	Balls	Mdn	Runs	Wkt	Ave	BB
1987-88	Pak						
1987-88	Aus						
1987-88	NZ	138	5	61	2	30.50	1-21
1988	WI						
1989	Aus						
1992-93	Ind						
1992-93	SL						
1993	Aus						
1994-95	Aus						
Totals:		752	29	317	4	79.25	
Country	Aus	186	8	68	0		
	Ind	96	1	50	0		
	Pak	222	8	96	1	96.00	1-17
	NZ	248	12	103	3	34.33	1-14
	WI						
	SL						
Home		294	16	133	1		
Away		458	14	197	3		

All 3 G's when playing together
Batting:

Country	M	Name	Inns	NO	Runs	HS	Ave	100	50	Ct
Aus	13	Gooch	23	0	710	196	30.87	1	3	8
		Gatting	22	4	873	160	48.50	2	6	7
		Gower	23	0	1225	215	53.26	4	3	9
Ind	7	Gooch	12	1	626	127	56.91	2	4	7
		Gatting	10	2	317	183	39.63	1	0	1
		Gower	11	1	451	82	45.10	0	4	2
WI	4	Gooch	8	0	491	146	61.38	2	3	6
		Gatting	8	0	56	29	7.00	0	0	3
		Gower	8	1	331	90	47.29		3	0
NZ	3	Gooch	5	0	268	183	53.60	1	0	6
		Gatting	5	0	170	121	34.00	1	0	2
		Gower	5	0	293	131	58.60	1	2	3
Totals:	27		140	9	5811		44.36	15	28	54
	27	Gooch	48	1	2095	196	44.57	6	10	27
		Gatting	45	6	1416	183	36.31	4	7	13
		Gower	47	2	2300	215	51.11	5	12	14

Results	Won	Lost	Drew
	6	8	13

All 3G's when playing together

Bowling:

M	Name	Balls	Mdn	Runs	Wkts	Ave	BB
13	Gooch	392	19	155	2	77.50	2-57
	Gatting	48	0	29	0		
	Gower						
7	Gooch	199	6	77	2	38.50	2-12
	Gatting	18	0	14	0		
	Gower	6	0	1	0		
4	Gooch	42	2	34	1	34.00	1-21
	Gatting						
	Gower						
3	Gooch	114	9	38	1	38.00	1-23
	Gatting						
	Gower	7	0	5	0		
27		826	36	353	6	58.83	
27	Gooch	747	36	304	6	50.67	
	Gatting	66	0	43	0		
	Gower	13	0	6	0		

Won	Lost	Drew
6	8	13

Landmarks: The 3 G's

Name	Runs Scored	Inns Taken	Achieved Versus	Where	Ave.
Gatting	1000	48	Pakistan	Faislabad	24.11
	2000	68	Australia	Old Trafford	36.08
	3000	90	Australia	Melbourne	38.58
	4000	121	India	Madras	37.52
Gower	1000	20	India	Edgbaston	58.78
	2000	51	Australia	Edgbaston	42.94
	3000	78	Australia	Brisbane	42.46
	4000	100	Pakistan	Faislabad	44.33
	5000	127	Australia	Old Trafford	43.22
	6000	147	New Zealand	Trent Bridge	40.94
	7000	172	West Indies	Headingley	43.21
	8000	195	Australia	Sydney	43.83
Gooch	1000	34	West Indies	Trent Bridge	32.26
	2000	65	India	Bangalore	32.35
	3000	84	West Indies	Jamaica	37.79
	4000	112	West Indies	Trent Bridge	38.29
	5000	140	New Zealand	Edgbaston	37.58
	6000	150	Australia	Sydney	41.41
	7000	169	New Zealand	Auckland	43.52
	8000	189	Australia	Trent Bridge	43.83

Landmarks: The 3 W's

Name	Runs Scored	Inns Taken	Achieved Versus	Where	Ave.
Walcott	1000	29	New Zealand	Auckland	40.74
	2000	43	England	Trinidad	52.25
	3000	56	Australia	Jamaica	60.49
Weekes	1000	12	India	Bombay	85.34
	2000	36	India	Trinidad	59.58
	3000	51	Australia	Trinidad	62.58
	4000	70	England	Headingley	60.61
Worrell#	1000	16	Australia	Adelaide	72.00
	2000	36	England	Trinidad	63.94
	3000	63	England	Trinidad	52.83

 # Worrell also passed 50 wickets after 33 matches at a then average of 38.38.

INDEX.

Abdul Qadir	66,67
Adelaide	38,63,79,107
Allott P	49,50
Amiss D	30
Ambrose C	68
Antigua	47,58,59,60,73,74
Archer AG	16
Arlott J	45
Amarnath M	61
Atherton M	71,79
Athey W	62
Atkinson D	17
Auckland	11,32,106,107
Bacup	19
Bailey R	74
Bailey T	14,18
Bairstow D	40
Bangalore	106
Barbados	3,5,12,13,16,19,20,47,60,73,82
Barrington K	45,57
Benson M	62
Binny R	61
Birmingham	17,56
Bombay	7,8,50,54,65,107
Boon D	55,78,79
Border A	65,78
Botham IT	34,35,36,38,39,40,42,43,47,48,49,58,59, 63,71,81
Bourda	6,12,73
Boycott G	32,35,37,40,41,42,43,45,47,50,51,76,77
Bradman D	7
Brearley M	32,34,35,36,37,38,40,41,42,43,48,49

Bridgetown	3,82
Brisbane	7,10,37,63,79,106
Broad C	63,66,67,69
Butcher A	40
Calcutta	7,50
Chandrasekhar BS	38
Chappell G	30,41,42
Chappell I	30
Christchurch	11
Christiani CM	8
Close DB	17
Columbo	51
Cowdrey C	69
Cowdrey MCC	17,18,30,31
Croft C	46
Delhi	7,8,50,54
Denness M	30,31
Dexter E	70
Dilley G	49,50,63
Doshi D	50
Downton P	55
Edgar B	62
Edgbaston	18,30,33,35,38,56,71,76,83,106
Edrich J	30
Ellison R	56
Emburey J	49,51,58,69,71
Enfield	20
Evans G	8
Faislabad	52,66,106
Fletcher K	49,52
Foster N	66,71
Fowler G	54
Ganteaume AG	5
Garner J	43,46,53,58,59,60

Gatting M	4,21,22,25,26,29,32-34,36,37,39,40, 43-74,76-81
Gavaskar S	38-40
Georgetown	12
Ghulam Ahmed	7
Gibbs L	15
Goddard T	6,8
Gomez G	6
Gooch G	4,21-25,28-52,54-81
Gough D	79
Gower D	4,21,22,27-29,32-43,45-65,68-81
Graveny T	17,19
Greenidge G	43,46,53,58,68,74
Greig T	31
Griffith S	5
Guyana	6,13,20,46
Hadlee R	62
Hardstaff J	6
Harvey N	15,16
Hassett L	10
Haynes D	43,46,53,58,68,74
Headingley	18,34,39,48,55,61,64,70,77,78, 106,107
Headley G	5
Healey I	78
Hemmings E	67
Hendrick M	39
Hick G	79
Hilditch A	55
Hogg R	38
Holding M	43,46,53,58,59,60
Hutton L	7,9,13,14
Imran Kahn	64
Jackman R	46,57
Jamaica	13,14,16,47,58,59,73,82,106,107

Javed Miandad	64,67
Johnson HH	9
Johnston W	11
Kallicharan A	43
Kanhai R	17
Kanpur	29,50
Kapil Dev	38,39,40,49,50
Karachi	32
Kirmani S	43
Knott A	51
Lahore	32,52,66
Laker J	5,17,19
Lamb A	52,53,58,73,75
Larkins W	42,44,51
Leeds	36
Lever JK	39,49
Lillee D	30,31,42,45
Lindwall R	10,15,16
Liaquat Ali	33
Lloyd C	43,46,53
Lock G	17,19
Lord's	9,18,24,31,35,38,39,43,45,48,51,53, 55,60,61,70,71,74,76
Madras	8,50,54,106
McDonald CC	16
Malcolm D	71
Manchester	44,56,71
Mandella N	72
Marsh G	71
Marsh R	30,31
Marshall M	43,46,53,58,59,60,68,69,81
May PBH	17,18,60,70
Melbourne	11,37,41,42,63,79,106
Miller KR	10,15,16
Morris A	15

Morris J	75
Moseley E	73
Moxon M	62,69
Mudassar Nazar	32,66
Nottingham	48
Old Trafford	8,56,72,76,106
Oval – The	9,19,20,34,40,44,62,64,69,71,77,78,82,83
Packer K	33,35,36,41,51
Patterson P	58-60
Perth	37,41
Pierre LR	6
Port-of-Spain	20
Radcliffe	20
Radley C	34,35
Ramadhin S	8,9,17,18,81
Randall D	33,37,39,40,41,52
Richards IVA	43,46,53,58,59,68
Ring DT	11
Roberts A	43,46
Robinson RB	62,71
Rose B	33,44,47
Russell J	71
Sabina Park	14
Salim Malik	64
Sarfraz Nawaz	34
Shakil Kahn	66
Shakoo Rana	67,68,70
Shastri R	50
Sheppard D	17
Sikander Bakht	32
Slack W	62
Slater M	78
Smith R	75
Snow J	31

Sobers G	16,17,18,81
Statham B	14,17
Steele D	31
Stewart A	77
Stewart M	74
Sydney	10,38,41,63,75,79,106
Tavare C	44,50,52
Taylor M	71
Taylor RW	39,42,50,58,71,78,81
Thomson J	30,31
Trent Bridge	7,9,18,20,29,56,62,68,71,79,107
Trinidad	5,12,14,19,20,47
Trim J	6
Trueman FS	17,19
Underwood D	41,42,49,51
Valentine AL	8,9,11,17,18,81
Venkataraghavan S	38
Viswanath G	38,39
Walcott C	2,3,5-16,18-21,29,43,55,57,81-85, 90,91,108
Walker M	31
Walsh C	58,68
Warne S	78,79
Waqar Younis	76
Wasim Akram	76
Weekes E	2,3,5-21,29,30,43,55,57,81,82,84 88,89,108
Wellington	33
Wheatley O	70
Willey P	40,58
Willis RWG	41,42,46,49,51,52
Worrell F	2,3,5-7,9-16,18-20,29,30,43,55,57,81, 82,84,86,87,108
Wood B	34
Woolmer B	31,44

ISBN 1425122124